Delighting in

Melvyn Matthews was bor
educted at Carisbrooke Gr
Newport, Isle of Wight. Later he studied
at St Edmund Hall, Oxford (including one
year at La Maison Française), and at
King's College, London, being ordained
Deacon in 1967 and Priest in 1968.

He has held posts in Dagenham,
Enfield, Southampton and Highgate, as
well as with the University of Nairobi,
Kenya. In recent years (1979–1987) he
has been Senior Anglican Chaplain to the
University of Bristol and Priest in Charge
of St Paul's, Clifton. He is now Director of
the Ammerdown Centre for Study and
Renewal.

Melvyn Matthews and his wife, June,
have three children. His other interests
include travel, poetry, music, the cinema
and France.

MELVYN MATTHEWS

Delighting in God

Collins
FOUNT PAPERBACKS

First published in Great Britain by
Fount Paperbacks, London in 1987

Copyright © Melvyn Matthews 1987

Made and printed in Great Britain by
William Collins Sons & Co. Ltd, Glasgow

To my wife,
June

Acknowledgements

This book was conceived during a period of sabbatical leave granted to me by the Bishop of Bristol, the Rt Revd John Tinsley, in 1985. I was given financial assistance during that time by the Diocese and the University of Bristol. I would like to place on record my gratitude to them both. I could not have taken the sabbatical leave without the active support and co-operation of my colleagues at that time, Father Leonard Marsh and Sister Pat Gower, C.A. I am deeply grateful to them. The congregation of St Paul's, Clifton should also be mentioned, not just because they did without their Vicar for three months but also because they have tolerated listening to so much of what this book contains on Sunday mornings! I also want to put on record my thanks to Dr Denys Turner, of the Department of Theology and Religious Studies in Bristol, and to David Isitt, then Canon of Bristol Cathedral, for encouragement and conversation. But above all I want to thank my wife, June, to whom this book is dedicated, for her constant fresh intelligence and total encouragement. As no other, she has released delight in me.

Melvyn Matthews,
Christmas 1986

What can we gain by sailing to the moon if we are not able to cross the abyss that separates us from ourselves?

Thomas Merton, *The Wisdom of the Desert*

And it more concerneth you to be an illustrious creature than to have possession of the whole world

Thomas Traherne *Centuries*

Contents

Introduction

Many of us, these days, experience life as a puzzle. We are puzzled, quite often, at how the world has got itself into such a mess, and how it might get itself out of it. We read the papers and are puzzled at how the gap between the rich and the poor nations has come about, and even more puzzled at how it might be overcome. We are glad when heroic people struggle to put things right, or when pop groups or aid agencies organize themselves to raise millions of pounds to help the starving; but we still scratch our heads at how a more permanent solution might be found. Eventually we usually think it's somebody else's problem.

But we are also puzzled about ourselves. We know, most of the time, that we want to be happy and good; but for the majority, just remaining reasonably happy is a fairly serious struggle. Goodness is something which may come our way once in a while. As for "holiness" or "sanctity", well, those things are for the spiritual athletes and the very dedicated, and we just do not have the energy to go that far. We might admire those who do, even envy them, but we usually settle for the ordinary business of keeping our lives in one piece where we are. This was illustrated for me recently when I asked my parish to attend a study day on "Holiness". There was a pretty shocked response. People would have been very happy with something like "Wholeness", but "Holiness" was really asking too much. It was like asking people to provide an answer to the problem of the divide between rich and poor nations. A bit beyond their reach. People feel, I suppose, pretty shattered most of the time, and want the Church to put them together a bit, but as for the spiritual reaches of holiness that really is too much to ask.

Whichever way we turn, then, there is a puzzle; and it's not really a very different puzzle, it seems to me, whether we are face to face with the starving in Africa or the problems of how to be the person we want to be in our own home. Most of the time we just feel out of joint. Much is required, we know, but little, it seems, can be done.

It is at this very human point in existence, I think, that most people find themselves most of the time. It is also, effectively speaking, the point of genesis for much of what follows in this book. Let us look at it, then, for a little while longer. Take again the question of world poverty. Many of us join in the activities organized by Christian Aid, CAFOD or Oxfam because we are deeply shocked by the imbalance of wealth between the peoples of the world. When we think about it this disturbs us deeply. But we are apparently unable to do anything about it except join in these various activities. We feel both guilty and powerless. We remain locked into a situation whereby we find partial relief from guilt in some activism, but are really deeply unfree to pursue more radical conclusions. The very same applies at the personal level. For instance, many of us have probably been in a church group which has talked, in an inspired moment, about the importance of suffering. We may have listened to sermons about it. But all the time that is going on we surround ourselves with various social mechanisms and behaviour patterns which preserve us from the worst ravages of life. We talk, say, about sharing, especially in parish life; but the resources of health and education in which we participate most of the time remain deeply unshared. I have no wish to criticize at this point, simply to refer to these matters as facts of our social existence. The Christian religion participates in this dilemma in a very real way – indeed, as soon as we profess any form of faith we are caught up into this disjointed state with a vengeance. We cannot escape. The practice of religion is deeply important to us, but the consequences of religion do not seem to come to the surface in any very concrete way. If they do it is only at an individual level and then always fraught with great ambiguity.

One answer, of course, is to say that we are sinful and weak and cannot aspire to the heights of perfection scaled by the Mother Teresas of this world. That is true, but it never seems to settle the question finally. Are there not perhaps other forces at work which actually put us in the position of not being able to scale these heights? Could there not be some sort of social captivity in operation which is in fact stronger than we are and which no amount of will power, however much aided and abetted by grace, can overcome? Are we not unable to do what our root being wants to do because our social existence actually removes us from permanent contact with those roots?

All these questions have caused me to wonder whether there is not an enormous fracture somewhere in our corporate existence – a disjointedness which has its roots deep within people and their social past. This is a fracture which makes us long to be something else but which permanently disables us from ever reaching that point. I have begun to wonder whether almost the whole of our lives has not been taken over by this fracture, so that we suffer from a sort of permanent nostalgia for the golden age of human and Christian achievement, but also a permanent inability, perhaps even a basic unwillingness, to reach it.

On the whole the large majority of Christian people should be given the credit of being aware of their disjointed state and aware that something must be done about it. It is also true that a certain amount can be done. Church life, for example, does help people to forgive themselves and to lead more secure, less fractured lives. It can enable them to rid themselves of fantasies about themselves and the world in which they live. It does provide the means by which no small amount of social action on behalf of the poor can be engendered, and it actually does provide a genuine form of support for many who would otherwise be cast adrift without any means of finding themselves as human beings at all. And usually it does all this with a very clear transcendental reference. But whereas all that is true, and is often enough to satisfy us, church life as it is still does not provide us with a sufficient basis for persistent *further* questioning about why we are like we are and whether or not something can be done about it. It does not actually tackle the very disease from which we suffer. If anything it provides reinforcement for it.

Nor are the economic arguments sufficiently powerful simply as arguments. I am no economist, but I have come to believe that the economic analysis put forward by the third world aid agencies is more or less correct. There is a total imbalance between North and South which must be corrected by political action. Aid and development are always being frustrated by the lack of political restructuring. Moreover, a considerable number of Western secular economists would now accept these arguments; but we do not seem to be able to follow them through. What we do need somehow is to find within ourselves an urgency with which we can pick up these economic and political arguments more swiftly, and do something with them. We need an inner motivation, some inner requirement which will release us from our fractured and dislocated state. And this will be an inner requirement which mere ratiocination and will power will not provide on their own.

This, it seems to me, is the nub of the problem. We just do not have that "inner requirement", we cannot release ourselves from our fractured condition precisely because we are within it. The way we try to solve our problems, both globally and personally, is part of the problem. We think about things, for example, in a way which implies that if we think about them clearly enough and find the right intellectual understanding, then something can be done. This is true. Things can be done and usually not enough is done. But the problem lies further back than that. It is not just thinking hard about things and then screwing ourselves to a rational plan which will provide the answers. We have to live with an understanding which enables us to see ourselves, and our thinking and willing, as part of the problem we face. It is not simply a question of finding answers and applying solutions in that way, for one of the reasons why the world is out of joint is because we are out of joint. If we can understand that then the possibilities become more powerful and the solutions more long lasting. It will then be not just a matter of giving people reasons why, for example, they should help the third world, but actually providing people with the inner liberation they need so that they can do nothing but participate in and identify with the liberation of the third world wherever it may be. In this way the liberation of the third world and the liberation of ourselves come together as part and parcel of the same movement. The "inner requirement" to share in the deliverance of the poor from oppression in, say, South Africa, is provided because we have discovered within ourselves that very same requirement. Only this sort of inner understanding will be of any use in the long run, because those who struggle for freedom merely for intellectual reasons will drop out or betray the struggle unless it is borne within them.

Just to be personal for a moment, I think it's worth saying that I discovered some of this for myself during a period of teaching in Africa. I have discovered more of it in my work as a parish priest and university chaplain. As we shall see in a later chapter, the condition of "being at university" provides a unique instance of the dilemma we are talking about. Of the young people who come up to university in this country, many survive brilliantly. Others find increasing difficulty in achieving a marriage between their academic lives and their personal desires. If considerable discomfort or breakdown occurs then they may turn to the counselling services or to the chaplaincies for help and support, but in no way will the academic community begin to think that these personal problems are caused by or even exacerbated by the academic quest. Nor will it easily see that the provision of pastoral help is germane to the proper completion of the academic task. It cannot or will not see that it is part of the problem. The problems that students and, increasingly, academics face are relegated to another realm of existence and labelled "personal". Chaplains and counsellors are there to catch those who have "personal problems", or who "cannot cope", in the hope that perhaps they will make them better and slot them back into the system. Too much counselling might suggest, I suppose, that there is something really amiss. But the intellectual will not achieve the goals of his intellect if the intellectual community does not provide him with the requirements of personal happiness. If this community is only concerned with personal achievement – and I have seen too many examples to know that it is not concerned with much else – then it is in fact profoundly irrational.

The very fact that the academic community finds it difficult to understand all this is a vivid example of that condition of being "out of joint" from which we all suffer. This condition, of which "puzzlement" is the tell-tale indicator, is one which needs to be resolved, not simply talked about or regarded as somebody else's business. The academic condition, however, only seems to want to talk about things, not to change them. This, to my mind, is only further evidence of that complete disjunction between the heart and the head which is actually in the process of destroying us all.

But this is only one side of the question. Whereas "puzzlement" or "disjointedness" is the primary experience, there is also a point at which human beings can recognize or be caught into a glimpse of wholeness, delight and total goodness which they know to be theirs and to have been theirs from the beginning. The recognition of this delight and goodness does impart enormous life and confidence to people and does set them free, not so much from the puzzlement itself as from the power that it exerts.

Some of my discovery of the possibility of delight came from my reading of Thomas Merton, the American contemplative. Meanwhile Thomas Traherne's *Centuries* had lain practically unread on my shelves since I was given it by a friend in his beautiful house high above the Rift Valley in East Africa some years ago. I devoured them now. I came to know that "delight" was our original condition. Original, not because it replaces or abolishes original sin but because it seems to me to be a state which is experienced (and by that I do not necessarily mean "felt") as behind or beyond the condition of puzzlement or disjointedness which disguises it. It is prior. The discovery of its existence is, to my mind, a question of "recognition"[1] rather than anything else. It has to be "seen", and it is usually only "seen" as the result of crisis or intense suffering – and not always even then – or in company with the delight in creation, in others or in themselves, which human beings can experience once removed from the packaged pleasures which Western civilization so often wishes upon them. This "original goodness" is often only glimpsed, but when glimpsed its effects are far reaching and long lasting. I have been told that all this is hopelessly optimistic, but I remain unconvinced that our condition of puzzlement or disjointedness is the last word, and aware that we have been given a prior condition to enjoy which we simply insist on missing most of the time. The Church, I am sure, is absolutely necessary to the complete recognition and the sustenance of this act of recognition in men and women. The eucharist is the focal point for this act or moment of recognition, which is why the story of the supper on the Road to Emmaus is of central significance. But I also think it is true that many outside of the formal bounds of church life do come to a similar understanding, share in this recognition of delight as our original condition, and allow it to generate a vision of the just society, which often the Church itself has lost. Such people cannot, for all sorts of reasons, put this recognition within a Christian framework, and so it is the Church's task, I would suggest, to seek to stand with such half-believers and enable them to see how they can fit into a Christian framework, and meanwhile to allow the Church's life to be purified by their vision.

It is part of the purpose of this book to help us do all this more easily and more frequently. If we can, then that will be a sign that we are living with a little more freedom from the great power that our contemporary sense of puzzlement has over us, and with a little more recognition of the capacity for delight which has been given to us.

And so this book is offered in the hope that it will provide some explanation of how we have arrived where we are, and some suggestions as to how we might recover that "inner requirement" to live other than we do. What I have tried to say in these opening pages is that our condition is a personal one, one that we all know about and live with most of the time. And so although this book contains a small attempt to bring to a wider audience some of the work that has been going on – almost under our noses – in universities and other places where people write and talk, it is not, in principle, an "intellectual" book. It is, rather, an attempt to understand where we are and why we are there, why we feel as we do and what we might do to resolve it all. In fact, I suppose it is an attempt to say how we might be saved, but without the jargon. Inevitably, it is a popularization of other people's ideas. It is, also inevitably, a work of intellectual synthesis, but it begins with an attempt to see where we are now in human terms.

I said "almost under our noses" just now because it appears to me that one of the symptoms of our disease lies precisely in this: that we have not, in the Western churches, learned much from Thomas Merton and others like him, precisely because the condition we are in requires us to tinker, along with the media, with such problems as the apparent intellectual impossibility of believing in the resurrection or the divinity of Christ. In the end I have come to believe that questions like these, which preoccupy much English theology today, are pseudo-questions and we are the victims of them. I say "pseudo-questions" not because they are not ultimately real, but because I do not think they can be resolved in the present climate. While we are "out of joint" we cannot but tinker. But once we have tackled the initial problem of our spirituality, of "how we see things", then we shall be able to look again at the problems of doctrine and ecclesiology which we now insist, wrongly, on tackling too soon. I have no doubt that we shall be very surprised as to what we will and will not be able to believe. We shall certainly jettison a great deal of doctrinal and ecclesiastical rubbish; but we shall also retain, with great commitment, a number, perhaps a small number, of very real and central convictions. But we cannot attempt any of this until the prior task is at least well under way. Meanwhile some brave souls, such as Thomas Merton, Nicolas Maxwell, Alasdair MacIntyre and Matthew Fox – to name a few of those who exist beneath the surface or who crop up in the pages that follow – have been working at a repair job on the Western psyche. Inevitably I have leaned on them in order to make my case. But although what I have written might sometimes lean on others it is written from within my own experience and in order to encourage and enable change. Change in Western society will not take place without understanding, and these words attempt to understand where we are, how we got there and what we might do to make ourselves happier and more delighted inhabitants of our one world.

Notes

1. I am indebted to the work of W.H. Vanstone, *Love's Endeavour, Love's Expense*, DLT, 1977, especially pp. 97ff.

1

The Recovery of Delight

Delight is life lived as gift. The discovery of life as a given experience is a discovery of God. Delight stems from the acceptance of what is, as good, and the thankful abandonment of any striving for identity. Delight then releases energy: energy to create, to overcome evil and to defeat disaster. What is created will be more true, evil more surely defeated and disaster more readily overcome when delight provides the source of life. Delight comes from a total acceptance of the gift of life. Gratitude and expectancy are its primary features. It is a discovery of and a glad affirmation of the fact that the source of our lives comes from outside, that we do not have to make ourselves or achieve our identity in any way.

Delight is always given. The manner in which this discovery is made may also be part of the delight. There is a strange movement in Christian spirituality in which the person who has abandoned or been stripped of all things suddenly finds that everything has been given back to him. Having accepted the loss of those things which were most precious and to which he has clung, desperately, for so long, he suddenly finds that everything he had ever needed is placed in his hands. It is returned with interest, together with a pleasure and delight in all that is which had, up until that moment, completely escaped him. This is a strange reversal, for most people have dreams of achieving certain goals, goals which in themselves are completely hon-

ourable and totally in accord with Christian teaching –
goals of sacrificial service, apostolic enterprise and so on.
The flaw, however, so often unseen by the one who has
conceived the goals concerned, is that these goals are being
sought as means of self-identity and not, finally, for their
own sake. They may succeed, and if they do there is no
doubt that they will have the benefits which are desired,
bringing healing and truth to many. But, paradoxically, for
the person who seeks their fulfilment it is often better that
they fail; for if they were to succeed there is the risk of
being caught in their success in such a way that isolation
from God is not only ensured but effectively reinforced.
We sometimes need to have success barred to us. We have
to be stripped of our attachments so that we may truly
delight in what has been given to us from the beginning,
namely the love and mercy of God seen in his body and in
the body of his creation. We are not without achievements
from the very beginning. The risk, of course, is that the
bitterness experienced in the loss of fulfilment will choke
and destroy the greater delights which God offers, and that
we will remain locked in a defiance of the universe. But if it
is recognized, however dimly and however occasionally,
that the pain of loss signals a proffered enlargement of the
spirit; and if the pain is not so great that the wounded one
can reach out again, however fleetingly, and look and see,
then we will find that everything is at our disposal and that
we may delight in it freely. We may also discover that we
participate in the delight of God and so can even delight in
ourselves.

It is this sense of delight which is largely lost to the
middle classes of the West. Its recovery is a matter of great
urgency. And delight quite simply means what it says.
Delight means taking pleasure in the created universe, in

each other and in ourselves. This delight, at its best, is quite unsentimental and totally realistic. It is a simple pleasuring in what is, in its strangeness, its newness, in its capacity to exist as itself. This delight is quite untrammelled by any desire on the part of the beholder to possess or dominate what is seen. It is unafraid of the power of creation, it is unaware of any threat that the creation may pose, it does not wish to protect itself from the creation nor to manipulate what is seen into any better or different shape. What is is good, and the beholder is content with what is and with his or her relationship to it.

We should not restrict the scope of what is. What is includes the created universe – and the beautiful pictures of Saturn's rings or Jupiter's moons which have been sent back to earth from space show that the universe still has delight in store for us – and the human person. The Westernized consciousness, preoccupied with a pessimistic individualism, requires, for its health's sake, loving attention to the complexity of human personality. We need to lose our fear of this complexity, and must learn to trace its outlines, as it were, with our fingers, as if we were tracing the outline of a snowflake or caressing the delicacy of a lover's skin. The fear we may have of this inner complexity is engendered within ourselves, triggered perhaps by what we do not know or by what lies hidden or repressed within ourselves. And as we trace what we are, we need gentleness and pleasure more than defiance or resentment or fear that our fragility will break unless we defend it. We need the same sense of wonder at the almost invisible complexity of our own beings as we have for the visible wonder of the created universe. The monsters we possess within ourselves may well turn out to be funnier than we expected.[1]

Our own innerness also needs to be the subject of much patience. Much of it is invisible even to the most loving gaze, and before we try to draw out or discern what is there we should ask ourselves whether we need to do so. Perhaps our urgency to know everything about ourselves or another itself derives from fear or resentment rather than love and delight. Delight requires patience with what is unknown and unrevealed, a confidence that if and when it can be revealed it will not be harmful but curiously beautiful. Such is the often unheeded advice given by the poet Rilke.

> I want to beg you as much as I can . . . to be patient towards all that is unsolved in your heart and to try to love the questions themselves. . . . Do not now seek answers which cannot be given you because you would not be able to live them. And the point is to live everything. Live the questions now. Perhaps you will then, gradually, without noticing it, live along some distant day into the answer . . . take whatever comes with great trust, and if only it comes out of your own will, out of some need of your innermost being, take it upon yourself and hate nothing . . .[2]

This is not only good advice, it is also advice derived from a sense of wonder at what is in store for us from the unknown, which is more difficult, but just as necessary. If we can learn some of this delight, practise it, being pleased with who we may be as well as with what we are, then we may begin to be happier with ourselves and more just in our political dealings.

Delight will involve us in strangeness rather than familiarity, simplicity rather than difficulty or complication, and "seeing" rather than hearing. Let us take each one of these in turn.

Delight, when it is true, enables us to enjoy what is, in fact, very strange, and to know something of the pain and difficulty that this strangeness has had in its growth. This strangeness is writ large upon the faces of those who have suffered great hardship. Much Western delight, if it can be called as much, stops well short of this strangeness, and packages a lot of pleasure in such a way that the struggle and the pain which went into its production is disguised or removed. We are sold music which is deeply detached from its strange origins in the soul and social circumstances of the composer, and turned into "beautiful arrangements". We are sold art which is bought on the international markets as an investment. Its "strangeness", and the delight which that strangeness may bring, has been lost in the deal. Western society hides itself from the aged who have, perhaps, some of the strangest beauty on display. Their beauty is evident in the way in which what they are now has been shaped by forces in the past that we can only glimpse at or read about in history books. Even the aged who are still angry with life contain hidden puzzles which will, with patience and attention, bring awe and delight to those who dare befriend them. Delight in what is is in danger of being replaced by an index-linked packaged beauty which is no more than another product of the consumerist society.

The great part of scientific research is rooted in an exploration, a delighted and wondering exploration, of the strangeness of the universe. Anybody accompanying a research scientist on a tour of his laboratory cannot fail to see this. The odd behaviour of nuclear particles, the peculiar behaviour of crystals at low temperatures, the unpredictable element in chemical exchanges, the relationship of stress to the behaviour of metal — all this is not simply a source of fascination, it is also a source of life, the subject of much discussion, comparison, recollection and, eventually, application. The majority of research scientists more frequently resemble children than ambitious demagogues seeking power to destroy the world. Their fascination is with the strangeness, their lack of interest is about the application. True delight learns a proper appreciation of strangeness.

True delight also relies more on seeing than hearing. It is a recognition of what is the case with things, a "seeing" of the truth from within. This is important because so much of our Western existence is dominated by insistent voices telling us what we need to hear and know. Different voices preach different messages, asking us to listen and "be persuaded" rather than taking us by the hand and, silently almost, showing us what can be seen. Persuasion is a dominant element in the Westernized consciousness, "attention" and "sight" have been submerged. The Annunciation, for example, is too often understood as something which was "heard" by the Virgin rather than as a "seeing". There is, however, a strong religious tradition which understands the Annunciation as a seeing, a mutual recognition of seer and seen, a moment when the Virgin is seen as she truly is and is able to respond fully to the truth. John Taylor, previously Bishop of Winchester, reminds us, in writing about the Annunciation,[3] of the Renaissance paintings of the incident which emphasize the enraptured gaze of the angel and the Virgin, with the Holy Ghost, the dove, spinning the thread of attention between them. Edwin Muir, the poet, makes the same point,

These neither speak nor movement make,
But stare into their deepening trance
As if their gaze would never break.[4]

This is delight. This is the delight which lovers know, and it is the delight with which we are known by God. It is the delight which actually waits to be released from within our illusioned Western consciousness, victim as it is of all the allurements of a packaged beauty such that we cannot see what really is the case, either with ourselves or the world around us.

Thirdly, true delight enables us to live simply. It is a delight in what is and therefore involves an acceptance of what is and a sloughing away of all that derives from an obsessive drive for achievement. It enables us to live with the regularities and simplicities of life without striving for the difficult, contrived pleasures which civilization offers. This does not mean a total acceptance of things like poverty and injustice, because those things are, in fact, irregularities, and a departure from what was intended from the beginning, introduced into life because of our tendency to rely on contrived pleasure rather than delight. It does mean simple delight in the most natural things and in the regularities of the natural – the movement of day and night, the change of seasons, the simple rituals of daily life. It means attention to the most simple ways of doing things and the use of the most simple materials in everyday existence. These things are vital for both physical and psychological health, and yet our hold on them is becoming increasingly precarious. Spiritual writers have commented upon this for a long time. Meister Eckhart says,

> Wisdom consists in doing the next thing you have to do,
> doing it with your whole heart, and finding delight in
> doing it.[5]

Thomas Merton finds, as have many others, this deep sense
of simple delight in the artefacts of the American Shaker
community.

> Marvellous, vast silent white open spaces around the
> old buildings put up by the Shakers at Pleasant Hill
> a hundred or a hundred and fifty years ago ...
> Marvellous subjects. I have no way of explaining how
> the bare, blank side of an old frame house with some
> broken windows can be so indescribably beautiful. The
> Shaker builders, like all their craftsmen, had the gift of
> achieving perfect forms.[6]

True delight relieves us of the pressure, the uncontrollable
need to find pleasure elsewhere than in the plain regularities of life and in the simple, unadorned life style
which we are actually capable of living if we would so
allow ourselves. Do we need the artificial pleasures of life,
when we already possess within us and within the relationships we have and the abilities we have been given, a
beauty that we need never tire of again?

The Song of Songs provides biblical illustration of the
nature and quality of this delight.

> "How beautiful are your feet in their sandals,
> O prince's daughter!
> The curve of your thighs is like the curve of a necklace,
> Work of a master hand.
> Your navel is a bowl well rounded

with no lack of wine . . .
How beautiful you are . . .
My love, my delight!'[7]

Jesus summons his hearers to a similar response to the creation in the Sermon on the Mount[8] and it has been a constant, if not a dominant, theme in spirituality ever since. Hildegard of Bingen, an Abbess living in the Rhineland valley during the twelfth century, who received a number of "Illuminations" and whose work has been little known in English-speaking circles until recently, writes,

> God the Father had such delight in himself that he called forth the whole creation through his Word. And then his creation pleased him too and every creature that he lovingly touched, he took in his arms. O, what great delight you have in your work![9]

It is the central theme of Thomas Traherne's *Centuries*. Traherne was a seventeenth-century cleric whose work was little known, because largely lost, until the beginning of this century. Philosophically he is a neo-platonist, but his principal contribution to Christian spirituality is a total optimism about himself and others. It has been said that he struggles for wholeness by means of "the recovery of vision rather than the conquest of sin". He asks men and women, simply enough, to abandon striving after righteousness and to delight in themselves. God's nature is to take delight in his creation. We are created in his likeness and so we shall only be most truly what we are when we too take delight in what is.

The world is unknown, till the value and glory of it is
seen . . . When you enter into it, it is an illimited field of
variety and beauty.[10]

For Traherne the source of evil and unhappiness in men
and women is ingratitude. This darkness will be overcome
by "enjoying the world aright'. He says,

You never enjoy the world aright, till the sea itself
floweth in your veins, till you are clothed with the
heavens and crowned with the stars: and perceive your-
self to be the sole heir of the whole world, and more
than so, because men are in it who are every one sole
heirs as well as you. Till you can sing and rejoice and
delight in God, as misers do in gold, and kings in
sceptres, you never enjoy the world.[11]

A similar appreciation of the importance of delight as the
key to a true spirituality has emerged in the writings of two
contemporary contemplative monks, Brother Roger of
Taizé and Thomas Merton. Both of them leave notes of
untrammelled appreciation of the creation scattered
through their diaries. Brother Roger is deeply in love with
the countryside around Taizé. His delight in the hills and
woods of this part of France is paralleled by his confidence
that Christ has placed a source of true prayer within the
heart of each person. The question is how that source may
be set free within the wilderness of European civilization.
Merton follows a similar path, delighting in the changing
colours of the woods around his Kentucky hermitage. This
delight is again paralleled by his evident delight in the
personalities of the other monks, and especially those of his
novices.

Both monks make the same point, that delight in the creation and in human love and friendship is not in any way separate from a desire for justice and peace between men and women. The link between delight and prophecy may not be broken. If prophecy is done without delight being its source then it will degenerate into theory instead of vision. If delight does not issue in prophecy then it, in its turn, will simply remain a type of privatized experience. Delight in creation will be the source which protects the creation from pillage. Delight in human beings will be the source which disallows oppression. Delight in self will be the source of compassion and forgiveness.

There is a similar point in the novel *The Color Purple*, by the feminist writer Alice Walker.[12] It is when the central character, Miss Celie, is brought face to face with delight as a discovery of God and with delight as the true source of liberation and prophecy. Celie is talking with Shug Avery about God. Shug Avery is a singer, a deeply liberated woman. Celie still remains within the power of all sorts of alien forces, including her religion, unable to see any worth in what she is. She says,

"You telling me God love you, and you ain't never done nothing for him? I mean, not go to church, sing in the choir, feed the preacher and all like that?"

"But if God love me, Celie, I don't have to do all that. Unless I want to. There's a lot of other things I can do that I speck God likes."

"Like what?" I ast.

"Oh," she says. "I can lay back and just admire stuff. . . ."[13]

31

The same theme comes through a page or so later. Shug Avery is talking now.

> "Listen. God love everything you love — and a mess of stuff you don't. But more than anything else, God love admiration."
>
> "You saying God vain?" I ast.
>
> "Naw", she say. "Not vain, just wanting to share a good thing. I think it pisses God off if you walk by the color purple in a field somewhere and don't notice it."
>
> "What it do when it pissed off?" I ast.
>
> "Oh, it make something else. . . ."[14]

This conversation is the beginning of a social transformation for Celie, just as the philosophy of "just admirin' stuff" has already been at the root of the liberation of Shug Avery. This philosophy is a deepseated doctrine of the creation which leads to delight, but which also inspires liberation.

The essence of delight is that it tells the truth, but we may be deceived. We will be deceived, for example, when we replace delight with culturally generated beauty. Culturally generated beauty is a system of appreciation which is produced by a politically and economically dominant culture. This system of appreciation, its values and fashions, then determines the direction in which human beings must direct their eyes. When this occurs, the dominant culture, often the possession of a few, is protected by capital and forces the poor of the land, the weak ones, to construct or discover their own sources of culture. The cultural history of all the so-called civilized nations is a history littered with cultural conflicts of this kind. As a result of this cultural appropriation by the politically and economically dominant culture, art, for example, or music, becomes a means of social identification. The art or music we appreciate becomes a means whereby people position themselves in regard to others. The contemporary interest in art as investment is only one indication of the way in which delight is now subordinated to culturally generated concepts of beauty. What is "good art" is determined far more by the sale room than by the eye of discernment. Art then becomes an instrument of class and, potentially, an instrument of oppression and division. In our age and civilization art has become a symptom of our dislocation rather than a means of its dispersal. The contemplation of beauty should lead to freedom and self-transcendence. [15] The difficulty is that the reverse has become true simply because of our predilection to transform delight into a culturally manageable and saleable package, a means rather than an end.

This has been noticed by a number of art critics in recent years. One of them is John Berger.[16] He shows us, in a very gentle and perceptive manner, how the way in which we approach art, whether as observers or as performers, cannot be separated from our other beliefs and attitudes. The paintings of Gainsborough are, he suggests, governed as much by "the special relationship between oil painting and property" as by a desire to portray the beauty of the English countryside. In reading Berger we are made immediately aware of the way art is governed by considerations of class and capital, rather than pure delight in what the artist actually saw. He reminds us of how the National Gallery sells more reproductions of Leonardo's cartoon of "The Virgin and Child with St Anne" than any other picture, even though a few years ago it was known only to a handful of scholars. But critics like Berger are also aware that art presents a problem because it can and does burst through the bonds of class and capital in order to present truth and delight to the observer. Sometimes this is done at great cost to the artist himself – Berger instances the rapid ageing of Rembrandt who struggled to change the conventional view of the function of art in his lifetime. Landscape painting is the least vulnerable to the claims of class and capital, since nature has not always been considered the object of the activities of capitalism. The work of William Blake also resists such an analysis because he too transcends, by means of a singular vision, the limitations of the tradition within which he works. There are "original" paintings with a life and meaning of their own which enable them to resist the alienating culture of their day. In fact, such paintings play their part in challenging and refining that culture. What Berger is talking about, in effect, is the importance of delight. One place where he finds this delight is in those few paintings of the female nude which have broken through the conventions of the artistic tradition simply because

> the painter's personal vision of the woman he is painting is so strong that it makes no allowance for the spectator. The painter's vision binds the woman to him so that they become as inseparable as couples in stone.

This is because

> They are no longer nudes – they break the norms of the art-form; they are paintings of loved women. . . .[17]

It is interesting that this analysis of the links between art and capital finds itself forced to make one or two notable exceptions – in the case of landscape painting and in the case of the body of the loved woman. These exceptions should not be understood as disproving his case. Art is riddled with alienation; but the alienation is not total. Delight can burst through and produce moments of true ravishment. Significantly, these moments are related to the created order or to the love which human beings have for each other. We may have to wait for these moments. We shall certainly have to prevent our sense of delight being captured by the machinery of the art world or the world of culturally generated beauty. We may at times have to go into the wilderness, literally and metaphorically, in order to preserve our sense of delight and hence our sense of God; but it will be worth it in the end. Reading the art critics one may begin to understand why the Desert Fathers acted as they did.

For the important thing about delight is that it tells us the truth – the truth about ourselves and about the world we inhabit. This is not only the natural world, although it certainly tells us the truth about that, but also the world of values and cultural attitudes which we inhabit. It tells us the truth about that world by exposing the lie that these values contain. It reveals their falsity and their alienating power. It "unmasks" for us the power these values contain to take us away from our true selves and give us the false, alienated, culture ridden selves which we like to inhabit. True delight delivers us from slavery. We are enslaved to false beauty.[18] We are also enslaved to a false subjectivism, an emotional affectation which in itself is a flight from the domination of reason and will. We have to be brought to our true selves by the work of the Spirit who delights in us and who, living in us, enables us to delight in God. We have, as the prodigals, sold ourselves to a false culture. We have to come to our true selves, to the truth about who we are, and return to that truth without delay. The means by which we will be able to do this is by allowing ourselves to take true delight in nature and in that which we love. What we will then see and delight in will not be beautiful in the received sense. We shall see ourselves as we truly are — loved, cherished, treasured, but also awkward, foolish and fearful. What we are will not be particularly celebrated but it will be totally acceptable. We shall see the truth about the pain we suffer and our vulnerability to this pain, but we will also see our courage, and our delight will be in both the courage and in the vulnerability. We shall know the truth about ourselves and the truth will make us free.

Notes

1. Maurice Sendak, *Where the Wild Things Are*
2. Rilke, *Letters to a Young Poet*, Norton, New York, 1954, pp. 34–5
3. John V. Taylor, *The Go-Between God*, SCM, 1972, pp. 10–11
4. Edwin Muir, "The Annunciation"
5. Cited by Donald Nicholl in *Holiness*, DLT, 1982, p. 106
6. Thomas Merton, *Conjectures of a Guilty Bystander*, Sheldon Press, 1977, p. 217
7. Song of Songs, 7:2, 3 and 7
8. Matthew 6:28–9
9. Hildegard von Bingen, *Brief-wechsel*, Salzburg, 1965, p. 126
10. Thomas Traherne, *Centuries*, 1.18
11. Ibid, 1.29
12. Alice Walker, *The Color Purple*, The Women's Press Ltd, 1983
13. Alice Walker, Op. Cit., p.165
14. Ibid., p.167

15. Iris Murdoch, *The Sovereignty of Good*, passim
16. John Berger, *Ways of Seeing*, BBC and Penguin, 1972
    There is abundant literature in this field. See also Roland
    Barthes, *Mythologies*.
17. John Berger, Op. Cit., p. 57
18. Nicolas Berdyaev, *Slavery and Freedom*, Bles, 1943, p. 246

2

Original Goodness

All that is is good.

All that is is of God and belongs to God; it lies under his sovereignty and participates in his nature. He, by his Spirit, dwells within it and continually calls it to himself. In this way he continually reorders it according to his original will, and continually replenishes its goodness. The blessing was originally good and remains one of goodness, a goodness always poured out on and within all that is.

 And so it was. God saw all that he had made, and indeed it was very good.[1]

The "all" of this affirmation from Genesis is as important – at least for contemporary men and women afflicted by doubt about themselves and the universe they occupy – as the "good" which it supports. The physical, observable creation is, at root, all good. Human beings are, equally rootedly, all good. There is no outer part of the universe and no inner part of the self which objectively possesses a moral status which is at variance with the status of any other part. There is no hidden element, either far out in some uncharted area of space or hidden deep within the recesses of the human soul, which is dark and out of control, deriving perhaps from another source of life alien to the original goodness. Most contemporary understandings of the universe, most contemporary ways of looking at the self, and almost all theological expressions of the nature of the fall since the sixteenth century if not before, contain a hidden and implicit dualism or Man-ichaean assumption from which we must, if we are to be true to the tradition, set ourselves free. The entire ob-servable universe, together with the entirety of the human phenomenon within that universe, both that which we know and that which is unknown, is at one with itself and rootedly good. The realization that this is actually the case is the beginning of spiritual wisdom. It is the beginning of wisdom about God, it is also the beginning of wisdom about the self and the worth of the self. It is this wisdom which will enable prayer, worship and love of God the creator. It is also this wisdom which, taken radically, will enable health for the soul, release justice and peace be-tween men and women, between humankind and the created order, and sow the seeds of reconciliation between races and nations. Above all it will enable human beings to recover a deep sense of the beauty of things and then, for this is what we lack, to delight in that beauty with the same delight that God delights in us. The recovery of delight is the most urgent task of humankind in this generation. Without it we fall into what is traditionally known as sin. With it we rise to participate in the very life of God himself. The way to the recovery of delight is a return to a belief in the original goodness of all things.

Moreover, this delight is the natural condition of humankind. It is that which we were given at the beginning of things by him who delighted in what he was making. It is lost, as we shall see, by our lack of trust in it, by our refusal to participate in its life, by our refusal to believe that we are "illustrious creatures".[2] We destroy both the original goodness and our own true selves by our in-capacity to allow ourselves to be the channel of the out-pouring of blessing upon this creation. Once we refuse to participate in that outpouring, once we refuse to allow the original blessing to flow through us, then creation becomes divided, conflict occurs and that which is ordered by love falls into chaos. Delight, trust in and acceptance of that delight, is the natural condition of humankind. It is natural because it is that which caused and causes us to spring into being. We are the product of delight and created to be able to return that delight. When we do, leaving preoccupation with self and the fantasies of the self behind, we approximate most closely to our original condition, and allow the delight of God to live in us, so bringing us to our true selves.

In the biblical narratives creation is that activity of God which recalls things to their proper self-understanding and to their true, "original" or proper condition. There is little in these narratives to give support to a doctrine of creation from nothing, nor very much which would undermine or contradict such a doctrine. Contemporary biblical scholars have come to understand more clearly that the emphasis of the creation narratives lies elsewhere. In the first chapter of Genesis the emphasis is placed, at the beginning, upon the activity of the Spirit of God which moves across the waters of the deep and draws order out of chaos. The sea, as always in Jewish mythology, is the symbol of chaos and disorder. The beast which dwells in the sea is subdued and brought under the control of God. The emphasis is not, as later Christian doctrine would apparently imply, upon creation *ex nihilo*, with God displayed as the power able to summon things from nothing, as a conjuror produces doves from hats, but upon the loving establishment of order in place of disorder. Creation is the establishment of relatedness, of dependence and interdependence. It is a work of love rather than power. The succession of days illustrates this. On successive days the different parts of the creation are set in relationship one to the other. At the core of this process is the word of God ("and God spake . . ."), who is the source of ordered relationships. At the centre God's word or wisdom continually orders and re-orders that which has fallen into chaos and become dislocated or out of joint. In the Old Testament the word or wisdom of God is the one who is constantly present on behalf of God, summoning things into relationship with himself and with each other. Wisdom calls things to their true "home", their original state, and orders them when disorder threatens or prevails.

> When he fixed the heavens I was there, when he drew a ring on the surface of the deep, when he thickened the clouds above, when he fixed fast the springs of the deep, when he assigned the sea its boundaries – and the waters will not invade the shore – when he laid down the foundations of the earth, I was by his side, a master craftsman . . .[3]

In these words wisdom reveals creation as an act of ordering, a process of giving things their true nature – usually called "naming" – and placing them in relationship with other "named" things.

A similar concern motivates the way in which Hebrew writers come to speak of the exodus from Egypt. These events were eventually seen as being a repetition of the events of the creation, when God brought his people, by his creative word, through the waters of chaos and destruction at the Red Sea and ordered their lives by placing them firm-footed in the land of Canaan. The Book of Wisdom[4] speaks of the exodus as a new creation or, more accurately, as a symbol of the creation. The creation was refashioned in order to convey the significance of Israel stepping out of chaos into Freedom. The same theme is repeated in the Psalms[5] and is then picked up again in Second Isaiah[6] where God creates a new way for those who are in exile. This new way is placed within the context of God's creative love and as a sign of his sovereignty over all things. Creation and redemption are never very far apart. Now, looking at the Old Testament with the benefit of contemporary scholarship, it is reasonably clear that the creation narratives of Genesis, although concerned with beginnings and so placed at the beginning, are secondary to the primary experience of exodus and redemption. Chronologically speaking, writings in the Old Testament about the exodus predate writing about the creation, and it is not until the time of Second Isaiah (c.539 B.C.) that a fully developed understanding of God as creator and lord of all things really appears. What is interesting is that when the Hebrew people begin to understand something of the effective nature of God's saving acts, both in the exodus from Egypt and in the restoration from exile, then the natural metaphor for this exodus is found to be that of creation. It is God who through his word causes chaos to fall back and order and beauty to be established. He in his wisdom is always at work re-establishing primal order.

The same is true for the prophets. They constantly recall Israel to that which was the case at the beginning. Prophets are those who have a vision of God's original blessing and are driven by that vision to recall the people to their primal condition. They, the guardians of primal memory, the stewards of Israel's unfolding narrative, insist that the people should not depart from their original experience of deliverance from the waters of chaos and the pattern of life which was laid down for them at their creation or recreation. The Deuteronomic writer, for example, insists that the people accept aliens because they themselves were once aliens but were released from this condition by the creative power of God.[7] Amos reminds the people that God is the creator God

For he it was who formed the mountains, created the wind, reveals his mind to man, makes both dawn and dark.[8]

The cry of Hosea is that

Israel has forgotten his maker . . .[9]

And in both Hosea and Micah the people are called to re-establish their relationship with God and his creative fruitfulness. In the peaceable kingdom to which the people are recalled, men and women, nations and the beasts of the earth, live together in an undivided original harmony. The original blessing of the creator God is re-established. In this vision

The lion eats straw like the ox.
The infant plays over the cobra's hole;
into the viper's lair
the young child puts his hand.
They do no hurt, no harm,
on all my holy mountain,
for the country is filled with the knowledge of Yahweh
as the waters swell the sea.[10]

Nor is the New Testament out of step with this vision. The simple but profound development is that Jesus Christ attracts to himself, in the gospels, the attributes of the word or wisdom of God found in the Old Testament. He it is who, both in his teaching and in his actions, recalls people to the original blessing of God. He reminds his hearers that in order to understand God and how he is they must stand within the original "created" dimension. If, for example, they wish to resolve their dilemmas over divorce they must look to what was the case "in the beginning", saying,

> Have you not read that the creator from the beginning made them male and female . . .[11]

If faith is at stake, as it often is amongst his hearers, Jesus points them clearly to the created order which is a sign of God's constancy. Jesus does not attempt to resolve lack of faith by encouragement to greater effort, but by the reproach that the faithless have not seen themselves as part of the creation. The faithless are encouraged to "let go" and allow themselves to be placed, or to find themselves, within the blessing of original goodness. In the Sermon on the Mount fear and faithlessness are to be replaced by trust in the creator God.

> Now if that is how God clothes the grass in the field which is here today and thrown into the furnace tomorrow, will he not much more look after you, you men of little faith.[12]

Gunther Bornkamm, in his study of Jesus, remarks,

> Again and again it [creation] is the undistorted place
> where man is, remote from all imaginations and dreams
> and especially from all religious phantoms, so that the
> listener can understand, in terms of the world as it is,
> God's nature, his actions, and the significance of his
> reign.[13]

So Jesus is the one who recalls men and women to their
place in the created order of things and who asks them to
trust in that creation, taking their place within it as sons
and daughters of the most high. They must be released
from the power of disorder by means of faith that, at root,
all things are well.

Faithlessness, in Jesus's understanding, is inconsistent,
for it betrays a lack of trust in the constant reordering
activity of God. This is the key to the incident of the stilling
of the storm.[14] Here is a story which gathers with it the
elements which are present within the original creation
narratives in Genesis. There is the storm, symbolizing
chaos, and Christ, who, with a word, re-establishes calm
and order. He thus reveals himself to be the word of God
who was, we will remember, present with him at the
creation itself. Jesus delivers the disciples and rebukes them
for their lack of faith. There are clear parallels, both in this
incident and in that in which Christ walks across the lake
in the storm,[15] with the creation narratives in Genesis and
the references to the wisdom of God in the Old Testament.
God's act of creation is the drawing out of peace from
chaos and the placing of named things in their proper
relationship to himself and to each other. It is an effective
affirmation that at root all things are well and belong to
God. Men and women, in order to have faith in God, need
to place their trust in the fact that this re-ordering is

continually at work. Christ, as the Word and Wisdom of God, is the agent of this re-ordering, the herald of the original and primal goodness of things, who gives us our real names. He calls us to share in his work of proclaiming and making effective the original blessing which God has bestowed upon all things. He gives us the same task which God gave to Adam at the beginning. He also warns us that this can only be done by trust and faith, by "letting go" and allowing ourselves to be drawn into the re-establishment of the peaceable kingdom in which men and women will live according to that patterning willed by God from the beginning.

This theme continues in the writing of St Paul and in the letters to the Ephesians and Colossians. In these two epistles "all things" are created in Christ or are united in him.[16] God is understood to be continuing his creative work, and the centre of this work is Christ, who is the head of the Church. Those who give allegiance to Christ are linked into the ongoing creative work of God. The Church is therefore instrumental in continuing the re-ordering of things. The people of God are a "new creation", a sign of what actually is the case in Christ, despite appearances, and a sign of what shall be when all is at rest in God. What has brought all this about is the death and resurrection of Christ. In his death and resurrection Christ has gone through the waters of chaos, has disarmed the beast within and so, in his resurrection appearances, is able to breathe upon his disciples the original blessing given at the beginning. The peace and forgiveness of the resurrection are the peace and forgiveness of the beginning-time. Christ has discovered this original blessing for himself in the "letting go" of the cross, and he now proclaims it as being available for all. In his acceptance of loss he has discovered the original blessing of God and so breathes the compassion of that blessing upon his followers.[17]

Paul's doctrine of justification derives its strength from a prior and underlying doctrine of the creation. The human person is "occupied" by sin. Justification then lies not so much in the judge's declaration of acquittal as in the acceptance by men and women that the occupation is not permanent or final. It is, simply, an occupation, and there is nothing basically wrong with the land that they are in. Men and women have to exercise an inner recognition that the territory of their person may well be occupied but that its true condition is "in Christ", and that Christ has been at work in us from the beginning.[18]

The key to justification is the discovery that although men and women live "according to the flesh" (*sarkikoi*), this is only because they have lapsed into confusion and their true, or "original" state is to live "according to the spirit" (*pneumatikoi*). At no point in his exposition does Paul imply that the natural and original state of man is evil.[19]

At the centre of human existence there is a createdness which is essentially good, an original goodness which was given by God at the beginning and which he continues to give in and through the work of Jesus Christ. Those who follow in the way of Christ and who take his death and resurrection upon themselves will be signs to the world that this is the case. In order for men and women in the Western world to find release from the bondage of their dislocation, they need to place their trust in the original goodness of things and to participate in the ongoing work of Christ. He it is who parts the waters of chaos in order that the original blessing may be known and shared. In this way we will discover the simplicity and wholeness of our origins.

Looking at things like this is not, of course, the usual way of looking at the creation. The mainstream of Christianity is far more ambivalent, not to say negative, about the creation, and the legacy of this ambivalence and negativity will be hard to lose. But there has always been a subcurrent of thinking which has been far more radically positive than the received tradition. This subcurrent, or "alternative", tradition surfaces in the twentieth century in, amongst other things, the ecology movement. This movement is the secular heir to a religious tradition, ousted by rationalistic orthodoxies since the eighteenth century. This religious tradition begins within monasticism and numbers amongst its adherents such figures as Meister Eckhart, Hildegard of Bingen, Julian of Norwich, St Francis of Assisi and Thomas Traherne. In the twentieth century the profound appreciation of the created order found within, say, the later writings of Thomas Merton, indicate that this alternative way is not yet dead within Christianity. There are others, like Matthew Fox,[20] who continue to recall the Church to a radical appreciation of the deep-down goodness of things; but it is true that until recently, such a way of looking at things has been predominantly a secular point of view. As we have already discovered, feminist writers of the twentieth century[21] are amongst those who have rediscovered the alternative tradition in their positive regard for the self. We shall also see that liberation theologians, and all those who yearn for social justice and a new creation in the political sphere, need to root their plea more thoroughly in a theological recovery of the place of delight. One of the reasons that such pleas have fallen on deaf ears in some circles is precisely because they have not been derived from a prior view of the creation as coming from God. Without such a prior view liberation theology is dismissed as mere politics.[22]

Such a way of looking at the creation contains within it a number of shifts of understanding which we should not miss. These are shifts

> *from* understanding creation as a making of all things by God,
> *to* understanding creation as a revealing by God of what already is within his understanding;
> *from* understanding creation as something to do with the origins of the universe in time,
> *to* understanding creation as an affirmation of status or actual condition;
> *from* understanding creation as being something to do with the manner in which things began,
> *to* understanding creation as being an affirmation of how things essentially are in relation to God.

Creation is, therefore, an affirmation of or perception about the nature of being, rather than a scientific statement about making or originating. This means that Christian people, if they are to be true to the inner meaning of this understanding, may well find it difficult to participate in debates with scientists about the manner of the universe's beginning, as if this was a happening to which Christian doctrine gave a private view. Science will discover various things about the origins of the universe, and doubtless all is not yet known. The Christian affirmation is in a different category. It also means that to be true to the creation we will find the emphasis on God "making", and so on our "making", less important than our participation in letting go into what is. A very strong strand in Christian thought has seen it as man's task to inherit from Adam the task of "subduing" the earth given him by God at the beginning.

This has led to innumerable disasters. We are rather to attend to what is, to listen to its beauty and to understand its intrinsic goodness; to know that we too, miraculously, share in that pristine goodness and can, by the act of faith and trust, be so re-ordered as to reflect what we have always been. "Making", as an attribute of God or man, belongs to our disordered and dislocated status. It belongs to the sphere of striving and lack of trust; it belongs to the sphere of achievement and its consequent oppressions. All that we have to lose. We can only lose it by allowing the original blessing to sing within us.

Creation, then, is a recognition and affirmation of God's primal order. A creation-centred spirituality is necessary to those who would escape the dislocations of the modern Western consciousness. Thomas Merton has a moving passage in which a number of these insights are expressed. He says,

> . . . the doctrine of creation is. . . that which implies the deepest respect for reality and for the being of everything that is. . . [it] is rooted not in a desperate religious attempt to account for the fact that the world exists. It is not merely an answer to the question of how things got to be what they are . . . On the contrary, the doctrine of creation starts not from a *question about being* but from a *direct intuition of the act of being* . . .[23]

He goes on to contrast the act of being with anxiety about existence. The first is a direct participation in the being of God and is given to us as a source of joy and growth; but man has turned from this and made his existence a form of suffering.

The real root-sin of modern man is that, in ignoring and contemning *being* and especially his own being, he has made his *existence* a disease and an affliction.[24]

Notes

1. Genesis 1:30–1
2. Thomas Traherne, *Centuries*, 1.38
3. Proverbs 8:27–29
4. Wisdom 19:6
5. See especially Psalm 74:14–17
6. Isaiah 40 and 41
7. Deuteronomy 24:17–18
8. Amos 4:13
9. Hosea 8:14
10. Isaiah 11:7–9
11. Matthew 19:5
12. Matthew 6:30
13. Gunther Bornkamm, *Jesus of Nazareth*, Hodder, 1960, p. 119
14. Mark 4:37–41
15. Mark 6:47–51
16. Colossians 1:6 and Ephesians 1:10
17. See especially Stanley Hauerwas, *The Peaceable Kingdom*, SCM, 1983, p. 87
18. Romans 8:16–17
19. See especially J.A.T. Robinson, *Wrestling with Romans*, SCM, 1979, p. 90
20. Matthew Fox "Original Blessing", Bear and Co. Santa Fe 1983
21. See, amongst others, Alice Walker, *The Color Purple*, The Women's Press Ltd, 1983
22. See Robert Faricy, *Wind and Sea Obey Him*, SCM, 1982
23. Thomas Merton, *Conjectures of a Guilty Bystander*, Sheldon Press, 1977, p. 217
24. Ibid., p. 218

3

Delight and Justice

There is a striking passage in Thomas Traherne's *Centuries* where he spells out the consequences of delighting in "this visible world". It is striking not only because of its total optimism but also because of the extent of the consequences he envisages. Delight in the visible world is the source of holiness and righteousness, it "exalts a man to a sublime and honourable life" and, even more, "lifts him above lusts and makes him angelical". He compares the visible world to a pomegranate which God has placed in the human heart, there to be the source of grace and glory. Even more, delight in the visible world is the source of true happiness.

It makes him sensible of the reality of happiness: it feeds him with contentment, and fills him with gratitude, it delivers him from the love of money which is the root of all evil, it causes him to reign over the perverse customs and opinions that are in the world: it opens his eyes, and makes him to see man's blindness and errors. It sateth his covetousness, feedeth his curiosity and pleaseth his ambition. It makes him too great for preferments and allurements. It causeth him to delight in retirement: and to be in love with prayer and communion with God. It lifteth him above men's scandals and censures. . . . It makes him to rejoice in a present, visible, immovable treasure to which the rest of the world is blind . . .[1]

Delight in the visible world allows our true nature to be understood and released. This in itself brings men and women into such a relationship with each other and with their creator that they are drawn away from the necessity to struggle and fight to preserve their own reality. By a vision of what has been given to them by God, and placing their trust in that vision, humanity is drawn by love and desire away from conflict, fear and mutual oppression.

In a later passage Traherne says that what is central to this whole process is a different way of seeing things. What is has to be seen again. This shift of consciousness is a life giving process whereby we perceive the world and ourselves in that world from, as it were, the other side. This new sight is also, at the same time, a move into a completely different moral realm. Behaviour changes as well as sight. In the third "Century" he describes all this, how his disillusion with himself and the world lifted, and how his fear of "dangers which might suddenly arise from the east" was dispelled. What dispels his "want and horror" is a realization, an act of recognition, of what really is the case, what is in fact the truth about things. This is followed by a glad acceptance of the divinity of what is about and within him. He gathers this together in a poem "On News". In this poem he describes the shift which occurred in his consciousness, from a state of continually expecting good news from elsewhere to a recognition of and trust in the good news that exists where he is.

> But little did the infant dream
> That all the treasures of the world were by:
> And that himself was so the cream
> And crown of all, which round about did lie:
> Yet thus it was.[2]

Although Traherne's work predates modern psychology it is "psychological" in that it involves a "seeing of the self". In Traherne the self is "seen" as part of the creation, bound up with the visible world and as good as that visible world. There is no hint in his writing that in some way the inner self is objectively the source of hidden sins, psychic sickness or unknown terrors. Just as the stars are God's work, so is the self. Nor is the self in some curious way distinct from the creation – it is just as much a part of it as a grain of sand or a butterfly's wing. This unitary and totally positive view of the self is one which has, Traherne affirms, quite amazing moral consequences. To refuse to see the radical goodness of our own being, to condemn what we are, is to stand at the source of moral failure. We discovered at the end of the previous chapter that Thomas Merton blames the ills of modern life on a desire for progress derived from, or associated with, a neglect or condemnation by man of his own being. This is identical to the insight of Traherne. Such a desire for progress has enabled great material advances to be made, but this only thinly disguises the inner conflict which generates it. Meanwhile human beings are still frightened, very privatized, and potentially able to destroy not only themselves and each other but also the whole earth. This process must somehow be reversed, and the beginnings of this reversal can only come from an inner recognition of the beauty and godwardness of the self.

Delight in, compassion for and justice towards the self will not, if they are what they say they are, remain simple interior virtues, clearing houses for personal guilt and dread. They will also direct themselves towards others and the created order. Delight, compassion and justice towards the self will, if properly understood and followed humbly, lead us into delight, compassion and justice towards others and the created order. A glimpse of the true status of the self is also a glimpse of the true nature of the cosmos. A cry for justice from the poor and oppressed can only be fully heard by those whose delight in themselves has set them free. The social oppression of others derives from a suspicion and hatred of the self.

This can be illustrated from one of the novels of the South African novelist, Nadine Gordimer. In *The Conservationist*[3] she provides us with a study of a man who owns a farm outside Johannesburg but does not live in it. He is a businessman, and his farm is run for him by Africans. He is wealthy and spends his week buying and selling. Because he is separated from his wife he also shares in the social life of white Johannesburg, having a rather ill-suited intellectual mistress and often making up the number at dinner parties arranged by society hostesses. At the weekends he visits his farm and preserves it, making sure that it runs as it always has. He has to preserve it at all costs because it is a symbol of his own identity. What he cannot see is the emptiness within him and the destruction which surrounds and ultimately destroys him. The dry and empty house on the farm reflects the emptiness of his being. His son is estranged from him and will not follow in his footsteps. His mistress leaves him, unable to swallow his views. He seems to be the victim of a sort of emptiness of spirit, a numbness which prevents him from perceiving and acting upon his own inner moral decay. Eventually the farm is afflicted with drought and then with extensive flooding. The water washes up a corpse and we do not know if perhaps the corpse is his. It is a very powerful novel and all the more so for being political as well as deeply personal. For the farm is also the land of South Africa, the heritage of blacks, but occupied, lived in and preserved for their own purposes by whites, whites who conserve at the expense of others and in total ignorance of their own emptiness and inner decay.

This points up our modern dilemma in a remarkable way. Intimately related to injustice in the state is lack of justice and compassion towards the self. We preserve rights and possessions, if necessary by power, in direct proportion to our inability to resolve an inner conflict. If we attend to the resolution of our inner conflicts then we will also find ourselves able to attend to the resolution of the political and economic conflicts which surround us. The reason for this is really quite simple. These political and economic conflicts do not "surround" us as if they were some other dimension, some other sort of reality. They are only the outer, public form of the same inner, private conflicts from which we suffer. There is no real distinction between inner and outer life, they are part of each other. We cannot deal with our political existence by reason and will and our inner life by intuition and emotion. This is a totally false distinction.

The public and the private interpenetrate each other. What happens within is borne in us by the conflicts of our corporate existence, and what happens publicly is often a vast projection of the tensions, fears and conflicts of our common inner existence. Privacy is sometimes a false world, a construction of the self to protect the self from its own conflicts, conflicts which, because they are unattended and unresolved, threaten to destroy us.

There is, therefore, a necessary parallelism between the resolution of our personal conflicts and our political ones. It is, in the long run, only when we attend to the resolution of our inner conflicts by delight in and compassion for our created being that the outer, political conflicts will begin to be resolved. This is not to set up the "interior life" as prior or superior to the outer, public realm, but to set as prior the necessity of delight in and compassion for *all* things. This *all* must be extended to the self. Delight in our selves and a refusal to project the apparent darkness of the self onto the "external" world is the only way our conflicts can be resolved. The distinction between an "internal" and an "external" world is a legacy of the eighteenth-century Enlightenment which we maintain at enormous risk. A spirituality of delight, therefore, is also a spirituality which is concerned for justice and freedom in the political sphere. A spirituality of delight is concerned to exercise compassion and forgiveness towards the created being which we know, ourselves. In that process we are set free and so find ourselves delighting in the rest of creation. This delight, when it is true to itself, cannot be limited to the individual. The expression of delight, compassion and forgiveness will also be an expression of justice for the world in which we live.

All this opens the way towards answering the possible objection that a spirituality of delight might underestimate the place of sin and tragedy in existence. This is far from justified, for a spirituality of delight actually perceives very clearly how both the human person and the visible creation have been spoiled because of inattention to their true nature. It also recognizes that this spoiling is endemic and deeply embedded, not just in individuals but also in people and nations. We are very easily able to slip into the strong currents of dehumanization and are, individually, not usually strong enough to release ourselves from the power of these determinisms. For that we require the strength of a corporate belonging which will keep us clearly centred upon the true source of things. Effectively we require the fellowship of the Church and all the means of grace the Church carries within it. These keep the attention of the soul fixed upon God and upon God alone.

But the major point remains, namely that the strength and power of the corporate delusions that men and women are heir to can only be broken and eradicated by means of considerable personal and social upheaval. A spirituality which affirms that at root all things are good does not therefore carry any brief for denying the existence of sin and tragedy, either personal or corporate. It is rather a spirituality which is far more realistic about the origins and nature of the tragedies from which we suffer and, in the end, far more hopeful about the capacity of men and women to work towards the resolution of tragedy. We are more realistic with this way of seeing things because we see that tragedy derives from a corporate collusion in the misuse of the given creation, a collusion derived from fear. This is more realistic because it accords more with the insights of contemporary psychology and does not rely upon an a priori or unargued theological view of the innate inability of human beings to be good or to perceive the good – a view which has plagued the Western world for far too long. We are more hopeful because we are not condemned to working totally in the dark. We are able to glimpse something of the original blessing and know that whatever happens this blessing will not be taken away from us. If we co-operate with God in the continual re-ordering of the universe and our own selves according to the pattern of the original blessing, we will allow our true selves to emerge and we will discard the false images imposed upon us by our capacity to live with illusions. We are called by an ancient beauty.

Nor should we be inveigled away from this way of seeing

things by unintelligent or misleading interpretations of St Paul and his view of sin. Paul sees the universe as peopled by invisible forces. These have traditionally been understood to be "angelic" and "spiritual" in nature. The "sovereignties and powers" referred to in the letters to the Ephesians and Colossians[4] are said to be those invisible angelic beings which, in traditional mythology, peopled the universe and brought their influence to bear, for good or evil, upon human beings. They were invisible forces which had to be allowed for, feared, placated or avoided. A more modern and acceptable interpretation would be to understand these powers and elemental spirits (in Greek *stoicheia*), as the "established" forces, the forces of our established way of life, the conventions and rules by which men and women live. We might call this the established social pattern. These forces are represented by the political order, by culture and custom, by the complex of laws which guide and govern our behavioural patterns. The "sovereignties and powers" are then best interpreted by the phrase "our conventional way of life" or something similar. There is some evidence for interpreting the words "this world", which occur so often in St John's Gospel, in a similar way. In normal times these forces are necessary and good; but, it should be noticed, they are not the ultimate pattern. When they are regarded as the ultimate pattern, as the end for man, they become an end in themselves. They then become dark and satanic and lead to death. It was these very forces which were regarded as an end in themselves and which, by being so regarded, led to the death of Christ. Bishop Lesslie Newbigin follows this interpretation of the powers and sovereignties in St Paul and points out that on the cross these forces were disarmed, relieved of their power, rather than destroyed.

... they have been disarmed by Christ on his cross (Colossians 2:15). The powers of state, religion, law and custom all conspired and combined to crucify Jesus. By this act they revealed their own insufficiency (1 Corinthians 2:8). They have been disarmed. They are not destroyed: they still exist. But their claim to absolute authority has been disallowed.[5]

This is a very perceptive way of looking at sin. In this light the forces of this world are ambivalent, they may become disordered. They are not automatically or intrinsically evil. The work of Christ is then understood as a re-ordering, a re-patterning of those forces which have lost their original sense of dependence and createdness and have assumed that they are the only proper source of life. There is a deeper, further pattern which exists in God, and Christ looks to that unceasingly and derives his life from it. Those who follow in the way of Christ are those who are called upon to be the guardians of this source of life and to stand against the powers of culture and custom, law and tradition, when these powers are given absolute rights. The powers of law and order do not have absolute authority, they are signs and markers for the original goodness, signals that the creation has been ordered by God. If they themselves assume a greater authority than this and claim that they actually contain the goodness of God over against everything else, then a process of disarming must occur.

The doctrine of creation affirms that the created order is ordered and loved by God, it is not its own possession. This affirmation has the effect, the very important effect, of "disarming" the creation. Created things have no force or magic of their own, they belong to God. This belief actually removes nature, including human nature, from a separate area of existence known as "the sacred". Creation is no longer peopled by forces or agents that have to be feared, placated or avoided. It quite simply is, and by being itself it is good and beautiful. Nor is it its own, it is God's. Creation is a single whole and it is God's. The development of this belief is a prime cause in what has come to be known as the "desacralization" of nature. Because of the affirmation that the created order is under the sovereignty of God creation is removed from a separate "sacral" realm of invisible controlling forces. Moreover this desacralized nature is now commited to the co-care of men and women with God. It is open to examination and inspection without fear. It is open to delight. It may be changed and formed. New beauty may be discovered. When men and women forget this responsibility or when they usurp its delegated nature, then disaster occurs. They have to work within what is given and to accept that their place is one of being co-responsibles. Total authority is not theirs, but nor is total and abject dependence. This position is very difficult to maintain, but it is essentially a prophetic one. It is prophetic because it speaks against those who would neglect the earth, just as much as it speaks against those who would usurp its riches for their own sole benefit. When either of those courses is followed then the "sovereignties and powers" which men and women have thereby unleashed need to be disarmed and brought back into a true relationship with the source of their being.

Laurens van der Post, in an important little book about the origins of racism in Africa, leans on the insights of Carl Jung to make a similar point about the way in which whole nations or groups of people can become subject to forces which are stronger than themselves. There are, he says, "inner necessities", which grow stronger and which compel men and women to act blindly. This happens, he says, when man becomes detached from his true end, what he calls,

> . . the spirit of his original contract and charter with life.[6]

He goes on to say about this "original charter",

> If man is at one with its terms in his conscious striving it raises him to great heights. If he is separated from it by the presumptions of his daily self then this mythological factor within him turns into an archaic force which blindly dominates him, using its great force upon him like a giant.[7]

Van der Post goes on to explore some of the ways by which we can be released from the power of these usurping mythological forces. He tells of the importance of living our "now" rather than our past, of listening to new music and watering the tender seedbed of a change of heart — all themes of a spirituality based upon attention to and delight in the creation.

Moving into the twentieth century we find that those who have stressed with great urgency the need to understand sin in social rather than merely individual terms are the liberation theologians of Latin America. In liberation theology the concept of sin is removed from a primary location within the sphere of individual wrongdoing and placed in those structures of social living which are the instruments of oppression and injustice. The unequal distribution of wealth, the perpetuation of master/slave relationships by means of economic deprivation, actions which undermine the unity of humankind and the unity of humankind with the earth, these are understood to be the primary instances of sin. Gustavo Guttierez, the leading liberation theologian, says,

> Sin is a historical reality, it is a breach of the communion of men with each other, it is a turning in of man upon himself which manifests itself in a multifaceted withdrawal from others.[8]

In a more recent study Guttierez says that to live, in Pauline terms, "according to the flesh" (*kata sarka*), is to live according to an idolatry. Human beings are weak, compliant, "occupied" people who have accepted the power of "the flesh" over their existence. He corroborates, from a totally different situation, the insights of Lesslie Newbigin and Laurens van der Post when he says,

> The flesh is thus seen as a power that acts upon human beings and that with their complicity – a combination of weakness and culpable acceptance – brings them into the kingdom of death.[9]

The remedy for this is, according to most liberation theologians, a turning to the gratuitousness of life, an acceptance of the gift of life so that the individual and his situation can be renewed and the social mechanisms of oppression removed. This "conversion" relies upon delight in the goodness of life and the created order, as well as upon trust in the promise of a new life. Man is made in God's image and needs to recognize that this image is within him,[10] that he is made in the image of the "God of life", if he is to participate fully in the struggle to free himself and others from the injustice and oppression meted out by those who live "according to the flesh". In this sense liberation theology is a spirituality of delight.[11] Those who struggle for liberation are those who wish to re-order things according to a vision derived from the pattern given them by the creator and re-creator God of the Bible. Liberation theology recalls us to delight in the God of life. Sin is a disordered condition of human relationships brought about by a failure to accept the gift of life from the creator God. Liberation theology is a recollection of what actually is the case with human beings, a recalling to first principles, a request to recognize that life is given by God and to delight in that givenness rather than try to appropriate it, possess it or claim that it is the possession of man.

We may even press the argument a little further. The result of this lack of delight is not simply personal faithlessness, which may then be allowed to continue, or be corrected in the silence and isolation of one's own being, but also a disruption of what happens in social existence. The poor of society suffer because we cannot discover the sources of delight, recognize them and open ourselves to them. There is a very close relationship between the doctrine of original sin and the creation of a society in which oppression is rampant. Doctrines cannot be separated from their social setting. The doctrine of original sin is related to the desire of men and women to establish excessive degrees of control over themselves and their environment. We would do better to limit ourselves to simple discipline, what Eckhart calls "the bridle of love", rather than establishing such control which will break down under the force of its own tension and then leave us even more guilt-ridden than before. When excessive control is needed and demanded, and, moreover, justified in the name of religion, then religion has simply become a prop for the powerful and a source of oppression to the already marginalized. This produces a spiral of attitudes where the existence of original sin is used as the justification for further repression. A pattern of self-destruction then results from which there is absolutely no release. It is becoming increasingly apparent that those societies (like South Africa) in which oppression is endemic, find the doctrine of original sin a useful adjunct to their social policies. Matthew Fox, an American Dominican priest who has written a great deal about the need to recover the centrality of the creation in Christian theology, suggests that the reason why original sin is so prevalent a religious philosophy, when the biblical evidence for it is so weak, is because it serves the purposes of those hell-bent on preserving their own power.

> I believe that an exaggerated doctrine of original sin, one that is employed as a starting point for spirituality, plays kindly into the hands of empire builders, slavemasters, and patriarchal society in general. It divides and thereby conquers, pitting one's thoughts against one's feelings, one's body against one's spirit, one's political vocation against one's personal needs . . . Blessing is politically dangerous . . .[12]

And he reminds us of the line from W.H. Auden which goes, "As a rule it was the pleasure haters who became unjust . . ."

A spirituality of delight involves a search for justice based upon a recollection of the primal order. This quest for justice is the same quest as the search for delight in the

65

inner self. It is also a search which, as we have found, stands in some contrast to the traditional Western view of sin. We need, if we are to recover from our difficulties, to adopt a major shift in our understanding of the nature of sin. This is a shift

> *from* a way of viewing things in which sin is understood to reside in individual personal acts of willed disobedience,
> *to* an understanding of sin as the unquestioned acceptance of social attitudes and the attendant institutional forms of those attitudes which derive from and are maintained by the divided, disordered and warring self;
> *from* an understanding of sin as deriving from an intrinsic fault in our inner structure as human beings,
> *to* an understanding which sees sin as deriving from a lack of sustained and wondering attention to what actually is the case with human beings;
> *from* seeing sin as a permanent and ineradicable feature of human existence, something which is going to happen to us at every step in the road,
> *to* seeing sin as existing only so long as human beings are not prepared to believe their eyes.

What our eyes will show us if only we would believe is a blessed universe, a place of wonder. It is only flawed by the refusal of men and women to believe that they, and the souls that they possess, participate in its blessing. Thomas Traherne speaks the truth when he says,

Delight and Justice

The brightness and magnificence of this world, which by reason of its height and greatness is hidden from men, is Divine and Wonderful. It addeth much to the Glory of the Temple in which we live. Yet it is the cause why men understand it not. They think it too great and too wide to be enjoyed. But since it is all filled with the Majesty of his Glory who dwelleth in it; and the Goodness of the Lord filleth the World, and his wisdom shineth everywhere within it and about it; and it aboundeth in a variety of services; we need nothing but open eyes, to be ravished like the cherubims.[13]

Notes

1. Thomas Traherne, *Centuries*, 2.98
2. Ibid., 3.26
3. Nadine Gordimer, *The Conservationist*, Jonathan Cape, 1974
4. Ephesians 3:10, Colossians 2.15
5. Lesslie Newbigin, *The Open Secret*, Eerdmans, 1978 p. 159
6. Laurens van der Post, *The Dark Eye in Africa*, The Hogarth Press, 1955, p. 111
7. Ibid., p. 111
8. Gustavo Guttierez, *A Theology of Liberation*, Orbis, 1973, p. 152
9. Guttierez, *We Drink From Our Own Wells*, SCM, 1984, p. 60
10. See also Traherne, Op. Cit., 3.58
11 The study of the Church in Latin America by Philip Berryman, *The Religious Roots of Rebellion*, SCM, 1984, gives evidence for this. See especially p. 22. See also Henri Nouwen, *Grazias*.
12. Matthew Fox, *Original Blessing*, Bear and Co., 1983, p. 54
13. Traherne, Op. Cit., 1.37

4

Delight and Loss

So part of the trouble lies, as Thomas Traherne saw, in our refusal to believe our eyes. We stand within a blessed creation and possess this blessed creation within ourselves, but cannot believe it to be true. The way to freedom is to delight in what we have and to turn away from the quest for more, in the recognition that we have, in fact, been given all that is. At several points in his *Centuries*, Traherne, speaking from experience, recalls us to the need to let go and enjoy the world aright, as princes and princesses of the kingdom who carry the image of God within them. This "letting go", or in Traherne's language, "being satisfied in God", is, he says,

> the highest difficulty in the whole world, and yet the most easy to be done.[1]

He says we will never enjoy the world aright

> until we see that all satisfactions are at hand . . . by going further we do but leave them; and wearying ourselves in a long way round about, like a blind man, forsake them. They are immediately near to the gate of our senses.[2]

This advice is curiously similar to that given by the Desert Fathers to young monks who came into the deserts of

North Africa in the fourth century. They were told, "stay in your cell and your cell will teach you everything". We have to discover the same truth and let go of the quest for satisfaction elsewhere, a quest which gains its impulse from a deep dissatisfaction with what already is. This is a Western sickness, a dis-ease derived partly from a misunderstanding of the nature of God ("He must be somewhere other than where we are"), but also partly from a misunderstanding of the nature of ourselves ("I must choose in order to be"). Traherne himself takes the first explanation seriously. He suggests[3] that our striving for God presupposes that we think of him as "a being compounded of body and soul, or substance and accident, or power and act". In contemporary terms this is to think of God as an individual being, supreme of course, but totally distinct. Traherne turns away from this and suggests that God is "all act, pure act, a simple being whose essence is to be, whose being is to be perfect so that he is most perfect towards all and in all". This lets us see God as continuously at work within all things, including ourselves and the immediate circumstances of where we are. We will not find him elsewhere, any more than we will find him where we are. We have to let go and let God be.

A similar inability to be "satisfied in God" derives from our insistence on individual choice at every possible moment. The gift of creation contains the gift of self-consciousness. This self-consciousness itself contains an ability to accept or reject what is given. Having been given the gift we feel the need, driven by different necessities, to operate the gift, and exercise our given right to choose and so assert our individual natures. We may be aware, in a strange way, that choosing is not necessary; we may be aware that we are not the source of goodness; we may even be aware that all that is necessary has been given to us and that it is good; but we are curious about the question of choice — or perhaps afraid that we will lose it — and cannot, it seems, refrain from pressing this particular button. We have to see if it works. This is increasingly the case in the modern age. We are taught ad nauseam that we are individuals in control of our own destinies, able to be grown up and make our own choices. The modern individualistic Western environment does not give us any easy release from the pressure to choose and thereby demonstrate that we exist. A spirituality of delight, on the other hand, counsels enormous caution at this point. It affirms the goodness of God and of all that derives from him, and asks us to consider whether choice is actually necessary at the point of life which we face. It asks us to consider that we may be choosing for no other reason than to assert our own consciousness. We need rather to "let go" and "let be". In "letting go" we will be given back our identity as people with greater pleasure and greater fulfilment than if we grasp at it by means of self-assertion. In the one direction we shall continue to reinforce the dislocated consciousness of Westernized men and women. In the other we shall discover a freedom which will release us to serve and to be and to resist the powers of destruction with a power and freedom greater than theirs.

But there is a great deal which prevents us from letting go of our quest for identity and greater certainty. The whole thrust of our contemporary self-understanding is towards maintaining identity and so towards seeing a refusal to let go as normative and good. We instinctively feel that if we let go and lose control we will be swallowed up by the beasts of the deep within our souls. There are, furthermore, a number of factors which make this process of letting go especially difficult during these present times. One major factor is that in the latter half of the twentieth century "loss" is very much on the surface of our collective memory. Most major European countries have lost a war or an empire or overseas dominions of various kinds. We are peopled by many who remember days of influence. We have also suffered the loss of a way of life which is now perceived to have been a life of settled hierarchical patterns. All of this is certainly a blessing, but is still perceived as loss, and this is reinforced by the many films, books and television programmes which feed on this sense of loss by delighting in the careful reconstruction of those more settled times. Considering the vast amount of hypocrisy, oppression and suffering which such times involved, our current nostalgic yearning can only be understood as an indication of the great loss that contemporary men and women experience at an unarticulated level of consciousness. The Falklands War is a simple, but tragic, example of an inability to let go because of the power that the myth of past empire exerts. Nor is this nostalgia for greatness confined to Europe. It is a major factor in the political atmosphere of America at present. Westernized nations are busy clinging to a romanticized view of their past with enormous vigour. A very great deal of effort, some conscious, much unconscious, goes into maintaining the self-image of the Western nations as righteous and strong, full of moral truth and beneficent towards others. But this self-image only disguises a great deal of inner terror that in the end others – in the shape of subversives or Communists – will come and deprive the West of its self-assumed right to possess the earth. Much of Westernized politics is little more than a device for expressing and reinforcing fear.

Many people think that religion in general and Christianity in particular are part of our heritage, and must play their part in preserving that heritage against the inroads of secularization. Religion must serve as a proper adjunct to an attachment, however illusory, to past values. This goes a long way to explaining many of the tensions which exist in contemporary church life. The hidden agenda in debates over doctrine, morals and the relationships of the Church to politics and economics, is the more profound question of whether we can actually "let go" and "let be". The real division is between those who cannot and those who have found themselves able to do so. The adherence of the "Moral Majority" in America to the maintenance of old-style competitive capitalism has less to do with a "Christian" analysis of economic theory than with the maintenance of individual power and choice. Public reaction to episcopal pronouncements on political events has less to do with the correctness of their analysis than with the question of who is in power over whom and who, consequently, may control moral perspectives. The desire for certainty in religion, for security in national identity, for permanency or settledness in cultural identity, all of these are strong factors which make the "letting-go" of faith and delight increasingly difficult to make. Yet it is the one thing needful if the men and women of the Western world are to survive with happiness and the freedom to love and serve God and their fellow human beings.

The life and ministry of Jesus of Nazareth is the essential paradigm of "letting-go" and "letting-be". He is the one whose attention allows those who call upon him to let go and live,[4] whose own death is essentially a letting go and letting be,[5] and who is soon seen by the Christian community as the one who did not retain his glory but let go and was made in the likeness of a servant.

Perhaps the importance of this whole process, which is by no means confined to the Christian religion,[6] is best illustrated by the letter to the Hebrews. This letter was written for people who were suffering from a number of the same problems as we are. These were Christians who, because of persecution or because of the strength of mediterranean pluralism, were tempted to withdraw from the engagement of the Christian Church with the forces of the time. Many wanted to recreate a style of religious observance which looked back to the power and serenity of Jewish temple worship. This is counteracted by the author of the letter, who uses a great deal of skill and learning to persuade them that a quest for that type of religious security is neither effective, nor, in the end, possible. They have to do without a temple now. Christ's work, he says, has the effect of enabling us to let go of such unnecessary securities. The interesting point about the letter to the Hebrews is that the author, for all his obvious learning, never uses this learning – as St Paul often does – to warn his readers against the dangers of mediterranean pluralism and syncretism. The writer is obviously part of the culture of the mediterranean world, and does not feel that the threat to the Christian faith comes from that direction. His learning – somewhat "bookish" and rehearsed for the occasion – is used to persuade his readers to look to the present and the future rather than to the past. They must exist within the real world. The real danger is not syncretism so much as looking backwards. That is the real weakness. It is not possible to recreate the past, the old temple is no more. Christians have to let go and trust in Christ who, now, is all in all. There is no "yesterday"[7] to provide the source of faith, for Christ is the same for all time. "Now" the challenge is to go "outside the camp", to admit that "here we have no continuing city", and to let go into the faith of the present. The whole thrust of the roll call of heroes in chapter eleven is encouragement to go on and to place one's security in God, rather than to look back or try to recreate what might have been. They have to let go and set out into the consuming fire of God.

Their condition was the same as ours. They, like us, were afraid of the death and darkness of the contemporary world. They like us were faced with enormous cultural and religious loss. The quality and nature of their faith would become apparent in their response to this situation. The inability to let go derives from the desire to cling on to what we know. The consequence is that we live with one half of our beings, with the reason and the will and with the light of the mind. We live too easily with the effects of the eighteenth-century Enlightenment, which placed reason in a position of supremacy within the Western consciousness, and have lost our capacity to trust all that we are, especially those darker "irrational" parts of ourselves which threaten to undermine what we have achieved and to prevent the achievement of more. The letter to the Hebrews asks that human beings, faced with this situation, reach out into it and accept the loss as God-given, discovering a richer happiness and freedom in so doing. We can do this because the creation is one and within the love of the one Lord. The goodness of the creation is the only true reality. Pain, death and loss cannot be separated out from this single reality. When they come to human beings they do not come, finally, from a different, alternative source to that of love and goodness. They come ultimately from the single reality of God. Nor are they unreal. Pain, death and loss must be accepted as the realities they are, but they are given us in the same bundle of things, along with everything else, and they will only be finally overcome when they are accepted as gifts — doubtless gifts to be feared, to be wrestled with, to suffer under, but gifts none the less.

Karl Barth spoke of "the shadow-side" of existence and so coined a phrase which has considerable significance for Christian spirituality. The "shadow-side" of existence is that mode of existence which appears at first sight to have a total reality of its own, what philosophers of religion might call an "ontic" reality, but this is only the appearance. The reality which comes to us as loss and suffering, and is genuinely experienced as such, is the same reality that also comes to us as love and blessing.[8]

If this is the case, that there is a single reality, perceived by men and women in different ways, then the way to liberation is to trust that what we perceive as loss is only perceived in this way because of our lack of sight. We are, in fact, too close to the reality of love; it bears so heavily upon us that we can only experience it as loss at that point. There are then two possible reactions — either to stand apart from the loss and pain, to reject it from our own being and so confer upon it a reality of its own; or to let go and let be, to experience the pain as pain and to await the moment when this pain will reveal itself as blessing. The Victorian poet Francis Thompson puts the same thought more dramatically at the conclusion of his poem, "The Hound of Heaven":

> Halts by me that footfall:
> Is my gloom, after all,
> Shade of His hand, outstretched caressingly?

It is at this point – when we understand the gift that is in pain and loss and are able to turn to the pain as gift, while still knowing its pain – that we are liberated. Contained within this moment is an affirmation of the unitary nature of creation and an acceptance of the total goodness of that creation. Evil derives from our inability to make this affirmation and from the consequent reinforcement of our own individual consciousness as being central to reality. This consciousness then, in its turn, confers upon our pain and loss a dignity of being which in fact they do not have. Once pain and loss possess this sort of reality then we assume the need to struggle against them in a fight we cannot win. The very act of struggle only feeds and reinforces the reality of the forces, now demonic, which we have created and believe ourselves to be willed to fight. The only way out of this is to let go and let be. That can only occur when we have learned to love ourselves and have compassion upon the monsters which, when we are faced with loss, rear their ugly heads from the deeps within our being.

"Letting go and letting be" is the beginning of personal and social wisdom. It is a wisdom grounded in a spirituality of delight, one that trusts all that is as ultimately good. Letting go and letting be does not occur easily. It may be known about, but it must also be appropriated. Letting go and letting be are inner attitudes which we will take into ourselves either as the result of pleasure or as the result of suffering. No amounts of intellectual persuasion, force or social coercion can replace the part that pleasure and suffering play in the growth of human consciousness. People are transformed by pleasure. They are enabled to "let go" and "let be" when they are given a set of interpretative experiences which are more totally satisfying than the previous set of experiences by which they lived. People

76

are also transformed by suffering. They are enabled to let go and let be when they allow that the pain they have been given is not a threat but a calling, a call to pass through the narrow gate into life. It speaks to us about ourselves, our needs, and calls forth an enlargement of spirit. It is experienced as pain because of our limited sight. Either pleasure or pain can, of course, cause diminishment – either because the pleasure is "kept" for its own sake, guarded as a thing in itself rather than allowed to perform its own work of transformation; or because the suffering is so acute that what it speaks of cannot be seen. In this case the suffering also becomes a thing in itself, merely a cancer in experience, and no transformation occurs. In either case the result is a deeper alienation because the self is being protected, and trust in the transformative capacities of experience is being refused. This is a refusal to let go into the healing waters of creation, a denial of the original blessing.

That this process of letting go and letting be is dark and painful is well known to Christian theologians. St John of the Cross knew of its painfulness as did Meister Eckhart.[9] Letting go and letting be will usually involve us in a dark journey. Those who follow it may very properly draw comfort from the knowledge that it is the way of Christ through the cross to the resurrection, but it does involve acceptance of loss of a total kind. It involves an acceptance of the loss not only of status or ambition, possessions and security whether personal or national; but also the loss of mental comforts, the loss of the security of theology, the loss of images, devotional customs, interior landmarks – total loss. This does not mean that these things then do not exist. It does mean that our attachment to them has to be abandoned and we have to recognize that they are effectively no longer of any use to us. Once we have lost them we will then be able to take them back, but as means, useful signposts only, not goals. But it is only at this point that we will be able to think and plan as human beings, secure in a realism about ourselves and our natural capacities. We will certainly not be able to see ourselves as religious supermen. We shall be content with what is given to us, with the creation that we are and the blessing (and the deprivation) that we have.

One of the most striking things about the history of Christian spirituality is the discovery that those theologians who have most stressed the importance of the dark path, the *via negativa*, have also been the theologians who have been most attentive to and appreciative of the creation itself. The fall/redemption tradition, which is actually a much more anxious tradition, appears when we look back on it to be far less able to appreciate the beauty of the earth or the pleasures of the body. It is as if the darkness of the dark way is also the darkness of creation and creativity. The dark way strips us of illusions and enables us to see the beauty of things as they truly are. There are two significant lines in the poetry of St John of the Cross where "attention to the interior" and "memory of the creator" are juxtaposed.[10] And it is known that St John was a great lover of nature as well as a great exponent of the dark way.

The classic instance, of course, of the close relationship between the dark way of devotion and appreciation of the creation is found in Thomas Merton, where an appreciation of the beauty of creation and a movement into a contemplative "image-less" approach to God go hand in hand. Some of the most lyrical passages of his diaries, describing the clarity and beauty of the countryside around his hermitage – especially those found towards the end of "The Sign of Jonas" where he records the beginning of his development away from the catholicism of his early days – are closely juxtaposed to passages emphasizing how God cannot be seen, and how man has to suffer the withdrawal of images if he is to know God truly. The journey into darkness is also a journey into a true appreciation of the beauty of things, precisely because in the darkness illusions about the self are perforce abandoned, and true sight is restored. Our capacity to see is cleansed, and materialistic attachments no longer give the apparent pleasure they once did. What is truly of God, namely his creation, thereby springs clearly to the mind and heart with pristine beauty; and, moreover, we naturally begin to seek its beauty and its refreshment because we know that nothing else can do so.

It is also true that acceptance of loss releases in people real energy for compassion and the service of others. Those who are deeply engaged in the struggle for justice and compassion discover that the dark path is relevant to them. Those who find themselves forced to follow that path, perhaps in spite of themselves, discover as they proceed a source of compassion and freedom which previously they had thought denied them. Until that point compassion for others and the service of others was a struggle, but once the dark path of the acceptance of loss is appropriated then participation in the struggle for justice and freedom begins to well up as it were from a source unknown. This pattern has been known to spiritual writers in the past.[11]

It has come to occupy an increasingly important place in the spirituality of modern liberation theology. It is now well recognized that the springs of liberation from oppression do not just lie in a recognition of the truth of a class analysis of the struggle for freedom, but also in a personal struggle to let go and let be within. The bonds of determinism are stronger than they were thought to be when the movement began and the experiences of those who have followed in the dark way have to be drawn upon in order to strengthen and to direct the struggle more surely. Gustavo Guttierez, who is deeply involved in the spiritual formation of those caught in the struggle for liberation in Latin America, turns to the writings of St John of the Cross in his search for a spirituality appropriate to the liberation struggle and draws explicit parallels between the two ways. In particular he finds the themes of exodus and trust in the darkness particularly important. The important discovery here is that within the night and the solitude there is no isolation.

Like the Jewish people in the wilderness, one travelling this road travels in the greatest solitude. Solitude, but not selfish withdrawal, is a central factor in every experience of God, for it is in the wilderness that God speaks to us: "I will allure her, and bring her into the wilderness, and speak tenderly to her" (Hosea 2:14). Solitude thus understood has nothing to do with individualism. Nor is solitude opposed to communion; on the contrary, it prepares us for communion and creates authentic dispositions for it. Without the experience of solitude there is no communion, nor is there any union with God or any genuine sharing with others.[12]

Guttierez directly compares this desert experience to the experience of those who would genuinely struggle in the wilderness of injustice to rediscover the true communion given by God alone.

Delight and Loss

What is true in Latin America is also true for the more protected pastures of the West. Here too we need the powerful lessons of St John of the Cross in order to learn how to stand in the desert. We have to acknowledge that "here there is no longer any way" before we can begin to be true to who we are and to the createdness of things as they are. We are, in the West, so much the victims of illusion, mostly self-created, that we are basically untrue to ourselves and the state of things as they are. We have placed ourselves in a hall of mirrors where our own image is continually reflected back at us. We have surrounded ourselves with our own illusions about who we are and what we can do in the world. We need to be stripped of these illusions before we can begin to live together and delight in ourselves, each other, the creation and the one God, creator and lover of us all. Deliberately, however, we set out to prevent, if necessary by violence, any attempt to remove these illusions and reveal ourselves to ourselves as we are, weak and vulnerable. We cannot accept our own weaknesses, we dare not face loss, we resolutely refuse to suffer. By so doing we actually stand in the way of the discovery of true strength, the gift of the whole cosmos, and delight in God. When we have been able to do that then our present fractured condition may stand some chance of being made whole.

Notes

1. Thomas Traherne, *Centuries*, 3.63
2. Ibid., 1.23
3. Ibid., 3.63, 64 and 65.
4. Luke 19:1–10

5. Mark 14:36
6. The Buddhist doctrine of *annatta* has distinct parallels.
7. Hebrews 13:8. See also Floyd V. Filson, *Yesterday*, SCM, 1967
8. See the work of the Russian theologian Nicolas Berdyaev, especially *Slavery and Freedom*, Geoffrey Bles, 1943, p. 254
9. It is interesting to note that Don Cupitt also makes extensive use in his books of St John of the Cross and Meister Eckhart, but consistently treats them as representatives of pure voluntarism or "hyperborean" faith. A reading of either writer will soon show that neither of them are voluntarists.
10. Poems of St John of the Cross, Translated by Roy Campbell, Collins, 1979, XXII, "Suma de la Perfection"
11. Matthew Fox quotes a number of writers including Mechtild of Magdeburg – ". . . let your being be quiet, be free from the bondage of all things. Free those who are bound, give exhortation to the free . . ." *Original Blessing*, p. 148ff
12. Gustavo Guttierez, *We Drink From Our Own Wells*, SCM, 1984, p. 85

5

Where Did We Go Wrong?

We have lost our capacity for delight. Our capacity to see what is before us as the gift of God is severely damaged. We see what is either as our own or as somebody else's. All experience is a matter of property. The recovery of delight, the ability to see what is as gift, can only occur when we lose our demand for possession and control and come to ourselves. The recovery of delight will spring from a recovery of who we really are. Such a recovery will not be derived from lessons in artistic appreciation or aesthetics, although these may well be necessary; nor from instruction in the nature of the gift relationship, although we will certainly need that as well; but rather from the discovery of our true spirituality. What is spirituality? It is not, at least initially, connected with certain religious or ecclesiastical practices. True spirituality may well develop such practices, indeed will have to develop some religious style as no spirituality can exist without an external form; but it is not derived from them nor does it rely on them. A true spirituality, which will set free our innate capacity for delight, is one which rediscovers our relationship to a number of inner or "hidden" areas of life. We have lost touch with a number of these areas and persist in living as if they do not exist, or at least do not matter. We are surface dwellers. The reality is that these inner, "hidden" areas are more powerful and more important than we would like. Ignored, the power they exercise over our lives becomes alien and anarchic, cut off from the light of day. We need to recover a proper relationship with them in order to be properly spiritual beings. If we do not recover our proper relationship to these hidden areas in our lives then the power they exercise will become demonic. It is often assumed that these hidden areas are the emotions, but this is far from the case. Almost the reverse is true at times, because actually one of the symptoms of our dislocation from our hidden selves is a massive emphasis on the emotions, as if a recovery of the emotional will, in itself, render us whole. The Romantic movement of the nineteenth century, something we still live with in many ways, emphasized the place of the emotions, but was itself part of a polarization between reason and emotion which began in the previous century. The dislocation from which we suffer is not so much between ourselves and our emotions, as between ourselves and the inner tides of goodness, virtue and common social objectives which flow deep within the human psyche, both individual and collective. Goodness, the pursuit of virtue and the realization of common social objectives are not simply achieved by a release of the emotions. Emotion may accompany their achievement, but that is not the same thing. Evidence that we have lost touch with these things is provided by a look at the way we actually work. In theology we begin with what is true before we begin with what is beautiful.[1] In society we begin with what we can afford before we begin with what is needed. In morals we begin with what is practical before we begin with what is good. A proper spirituality has the task of reversing these patterns and reuniting us with the inner tides of beauty, truth and goodness from which our modern existence has separated us.

Some attempts are being made to bind us back together as human beings. Some of these attempts come from quarters where we might expect it, from our poets and from some of our novelists.[2] Other attempts have been made by twentieth-century contemplatives, especially Thomas Merton who observed the effects of modern dislocation with an acute but lyrical eye and pen.[3] Now further attempts are coming from a number of philosophical and academic moralists who are seeking to reconstruct a tradition based on the idea of common virtues.[4] At the social level the peace movement, the feminist movement, ecologists and those concerned with the economic dislocation between the West and the third world are all part of the same attempt to reunite us with the beauty and goodness that our inner beings possess. This is a return to an earlier vision, a vision of what is good and what is good for us all. Our capacity for delight will in itself then return as our true spirituality reasserts itself.

The use of the phrase "earlier vision" implies that there was a golden age when we were not cut off from our inner lives, an age when there was a universal agreement between men and women about what was the common good, when we did not live with parts of ourselves or simply with our own preferences as if they were the only good. In such an age capricious interest, curiosity, whimsy and intellectual titilation would be understood to be nothing more, or less, than what they are. How and when did we lose this earlier vision? Did it even exist? At what point and for what reasons did it disappear? Perhaps some of our questions might be answered by a look at history.

There is a considerable degree of interest in this question by those who are historians of spirituality. This interest provides not so much absolute agreement in detail as enough of a consensus to provide something of an explanation of how we came to our present position, and so some clues as to how a reconstruction of a proper spirituality might now be possible. For example, one overview[5] of the development of European spirituality traces the origins of our dislocation as far back as the late Middle Ages. At that time, so the argument goes, rationalism was in the ascendancy. This influenced the religious life to such an extent that theology began to develop as a static analytical discipline. It became more and more possible to be a theologian but to be isolated from the whole business of Christian living. Christian life and devotion then became in their turn things private and personal, outside the realm of rational discussion.[6] The development of theology as a discipline was accompanied by a very deep pessimism concerning the possibility of reason or intellect being a source of *religious* knowledge. All certain knowledge had to derive from sense experience. Certainty for the life of faith could then only derive from a number of clear sources – the authoritative declarations of the Church, the emotional life or perhaps the centrality of the human will. The Christian faith then became something which was believed because of its source in one or other of those authorities – it was declared to be true by the Church, experienced as true by the person or perhaps willed as true by the individual or the group.

Two theologians in particular reinforced this view. William of Occam developed the concept of religious knowledge as assent to authoritatively revealed propositions, and Duns Scotus was the theologian of the human will. The result was a disaster. For more or less everybody talk about faith and how it was discovered was then taken away from the human intellect. Intellectual activity, what we would call thinking, could not help believing. It was not surprising, therefore, that within the community of the faithful subjective experience became the order of the day, and there was a flowering of emotional mysticism all across late medieval Europe. This means that the so-called "Reformation" of the fifteenth and sixteenth centuries was actually more of a continuation of the late medieval world rather than, as is usually thought, a rupture with it. Martin Luther was deeply imbued with the philosophy of William of Occam, while Calvin certainly placed the will at the centre of his theological schema. Both were deeply pessimistic about the possibility of human thinking being able to attain any sure religious knowledge. Revelation became all. So the Reformation was not the source of a privatized view of religion, but confirmed in a very powerful way an already existing view that religion was a private and individual affair, and locked it away with the aid of increased personal wealth and the power of the princely states which came to the support of the newly rich, religiously privatized, individual.

Another, similar overview complements the first.[7] On this interpretation there was, in the late Middle Ages, a distinct shift in the way in which prayer was understood and practised in western Europe, a shift which is connected to a shift in theological understanding. At the beginning of the Middle Ages talk about "the spiritual life" was, quite simply, talk about life and how it was filled with grace by God. But by the end of the Middle Ages it was possible to say that some Christians were "spiritual" while others, by implication, were not. Being "spiritual" was a private minority interest of a few, intense souls. The spiritual life was judged not so much by fidelity to the Gospel as by the intensity, or the "religiousness" of the feeling experienced.[8] This shift was accompanied by a shift in understanding prayer. During the Middle Ages the importance of "reading" in the monastic or Christian life diminished. "Meditation", by which was meant ruminating over the words of scripture and so absorbing them into one's way of life, lost ground to "contemplation" in the sense of an interior emotional experience of God's love in Jesus. Prayer as petition lost ground to something called "mental prayer", in which the important element was the relish with which the soul recollects God. Prayer came to mean more a stirring of the heart towards God, and contemplation became a more emotional procedure. At the same time the links between prayer and action became very attenuated. "Rapture" and other sorts of spiritual inebriation became increasingly important. This was a definite shift in spirituality or in "a way of viewing things"[9] which was to leave its mark on the Christianity of Europe for a long time to come.

So the historians of the history of spirituality find that there was a distinct change in the way things were viewed by European Christians by the end of the Middle Ages. This was a change which involved a deep pessimism about the capacity of the human intellect to bring men to a knowledge of God and a corresponding enthronement of the individual will or the emotions or some notion of "authority" or "revelation" at the centre of things. Religion and prayer became private emotional experiences. These emphases certainly broke with the earlier understandings of the monastic theologians, and were quite different to the "way of viewing things" held by, say, Thomas Aquinas. The earlier writers linked the life of the mind to the love of God in a very close way and knew only too well that the will and the emotions were flawed instruments. But whenever or however it occurred there is general agreement that by the end of the seventeenth century the break was complete.

Just of late the truth of these historical analyses has been given support by others working in a completely different area. Moral philosophers, or some of them, have begun again the ancient quest for what is good. Amongst them is Alasdair MacIntyre.[10] Although MacIntyre does not trace the origins of our dislocation as far back as the later Middle Ages, he is quite clear that the seeds of that dislocation were sown well before the eighteenth century, when, for him, the crucial developments occurred.

MacIntyre is concerned to re-establish our ability to talk about moral values, about "good" and "virtue" for example, in a way which can be commonly understood and recognized by all. He feels that we have lost that capacity because of the growth in importance of an individualist morality. He calls this "emotivism" because it reduces the common good to mere patterns of individual preference. He argues that Western civilization no longer has a coherent set of ends. Men and women are cut off from the substance of the moral life even though they still claim to know, each one of them, what morality dictates. Imagine, he says, that the natural sciences were to suffer the effects of a catastrophe and that all we were to possess of the achievements we now acclaim would be a few fragments, half chapters, single pages. One can imagine the result. People would walk about talking about such things as "mass", "neutrino" and "specific gravity", but without the beliefs which were presupposed by the original use of these expressions. Their application, therefore, would be entirely arbitrary, and various subjectivist theories of science would clash in the market place. This, he says, is what has actually happened to our understanding of morality.

We possess the simulacra of morality, we continue to use many of the key expressions. But we have — very largely, if not entirely — lost our comprehension of morality.[11]

MacIntyre blames this state of affairs on what he calls "emotivism", a way of viewing things in which the individual reigns supreme and is asked to make up his or her mind about the situation he or she faces, as if all the criteria for the making of moral decisions were contained within each human person and as if each human person could stand aside or float above the situation in which they found themselves and judge it objectively. The net result of this is that all moral argument becomes rationally interminable. No moral disagreement can actually be resolved simply because all moral judgements are understood by us modern emotivists to be

> *nothing but* expressions of preference, expressions of attitude or feeling, insofar as they are moral or evaluative in character.[12]

We might use the language of objective moral standards and we might well argue as if we believed that objective moral standards exist and can be appealed to, but at the end of the day we can find no resolution to our arguments precisely because we do not, at rock bottom, have any common morality to which we may appeal. It is all a matter of preference.

This state of affairs is traced, in England at least, to the influence of Moore and the Bloomsbury set, and MacIntyre alleges that we now live in a specifically emotivist culture. He argues that such a situation places a totally intolerable burden on the individual and is, moreover, a mistaken analysis not only of the individual but also of the nature of morality. The result is that we are in a very disordered situation, always on the edge of violence, always yearning for moral absolutes of one kind or another, always fighting to have our own absolutes accepted by others but lacking the normal means of persuasion; always trying, and always failing, to "get it right". We are actually unable to reconcile opposing points of view, for

> the specifically modern self, the self that I have called emotivist, finds no limits set to that on which it may pass judgement, for such limits could only derive from rational criteria for evaluation and, as we have seen, the emotivist self lacks any such criteria. Everything may be criticized from whatever standpoint the self has adopted, including the self's choice of standpoint to adopt.[13]

The phenomenon which MacIntyre describes in social and moral terms is the same phenomenon which we have been describing in spiritual and religious terms. The importance of MacIntyre's contribution is that he sees just how all-pervasive the separation of human beings from their substance has become. It affects not only our religious but also our moral life. In the end it goes on to colour all of our social dealings, and generates an atmosphere in Western civilized nations of total confusion. In the end, all of our arguments about morality, politics, social policy, economics even, are mirror images one of the other. They derive, whether they are labelled "left wing" or "right wing" or "centrist", from the self-same attempt to reconcile the enormous growth of individual freedom with a certain amount of social order. They are all arguments produced by the rise of individualist emotivism. At the moment we cannot settle these arguments on their own, we are simply arguing against mirror images of ourselves. We require an external reference, but we have thrown away any belief that such a reference exists.

So where did we go wrong? This brief survey of the history of European spirituality together with the analysis of moral development provided by people like Alasdair MacIntyre, indicates something of an answer. We began to go wrong at that point in European history when we slipped into the mistake of denying the human intellect its natural capacity for religious understanding. We denied our true humanity when we dissociated the intellect from the religious life. Religion, prayer, belief, and, indeed, human morality then had to be understood and judged by other means. Some chose authority, others chose emotion. The net result was a clear separation of powers. We separated the heart from the head and then implied that religious understanding could only really be acquired by the former. Religion became a separate matter, a compartment of life rather than an attitude to the whole of life. Any regulation "the heart" required, particularly if it began to go out of control, could then only be provided by the authority of the Church or the Bible. Some even claimed that it needed no regulation and that it provided its own authority. Thinking is excluded. We were left holding in our hands an intellect without a home, intelligence as a thing to examine or appraise. Such an intellect has no purpose outside of itself. It is unable to relate to any goals or ends outside of itself. It is stranded on the beach of Western culture, unable to breathe. MacIntyre's view is that the place of reason remained reasonably intact until different varieties of Protestants and Jansenist Catholics had their way with it, saying that it participated in man's fallen nature.

> Reason can supply, so these new theologians assert, *no* genuine comprehension of man's true end; that power of reason was destroyed by the fall of man. . . . now reason is powerless to correct our passions. . . .[14]

And so the damage was done. We still live with the results.

So the explanation unfolds. The eighteenth-century Enlightenment, with all of its proclamation of the power of reason to lead men and women into freedom, was actually based upon a scepticism about the capacity of reason to speak of the true end, or even of any end, of man. Whereas in everyday discourse we do reason about our ends, and claim that certain moral judgements are true or false as over against others, in practice this disguises a fundamental inability to give any clear and universal status to these judgements. They are expressions of personal preference, expressions of the emotivist self. When the Enlightenment, freed from the restraints of metaphysics and the social hierarchies which were seen to embody those metaphysics, enthroned the individual as supreme, then European man was left with nothing but a tangle of personal preferences, or a moral outlook on life grounded in his own view alone of what would be useful or fulfilling. These preferences took on different titles, such as utilitarianism, pragmatism or intuitionism, but tangled and preferential they remained. In this tangle of personal preference only one thing, ultimately, was able to save the day, and that was power. Reason is lost, emotion is private, authority is discredited. Only power remains.[15] In the nineteenth and twentieth centuries the dominant goal for humankind is set by those whose power is such that *their* goals become supreme. It is becoming more and more clear every day that the modern world is hardly able to live with these consequences without actually destroying itself.

All this brings us back to where we began – to the loss of our true spirituality. We have become creatures of the surface, out of touch with our depths. We are now creatures of reason, giving total authority to the pursuit of knowledge; or creatures of emotion, believing that the only real truth is in the free expression of emotion; or creatures of authority, accepting the authority of the status quo, or the authority of our own culture (usually that of two or three generations ago) or simply that of the most powerful force around. All of these creatures exist together and conflict within us or within our group or within our nation. Such conflicts are ultimately irresolvable because they are not more than statements of how some people live. No rational criteria for authority or reason or emotion are adduced, people simply choose, or allow themselves to be carried along by the strongest forces available. They become proponents of a particular way, and defend it by wealth or by violence or by a combination of the two. For some each way can become a total world, a "place" where who or what they are is not given by inner conviction but by the company they keep, the symbols they carry and the clothes they wear. The inner life is non existent, replaced by social patterning, a carapace reinforced by fear of collapse.

In this twilight world delight hardly exists. It is reduced to a vestige of its true self. It become a useless activity, the property of eccentric individual hobbyists, amateur artists, birdwatchers, flower arrangers and origami specialists. Delight is reduced to a matter of individual taste, nothing much to do with religion or God, nor for that matter of any real benefit to mankind. It is too personal to be useful.

But even in its reduced form it is a sign, a rumour, of a larger reality. The impasse we have reached can be overcome by a movement of delight. Such a movement of delight, a reach of the soul towards beauty, brings the human person back into a unity with itself. It binds up our dislocation and ties us back into the creation. It is not an irrational movement because it includes reason; nor is it opposed to the emotional; nor does it despise the authority of the past. It is what it claims to be, a movement of delight, an act of attention to beauty which overcomes division and ties the soul to God. Once we allow this movement to occur then we shall reunite ourselves with the inner streams of goodness and truth which flow within us. We must allow ourselves to be called by an ancient beauty.

Notes

1. See Hans Urs von Balthazar, *The Glory of the Lord*, T. & T. Clark, 1932, Vol. 1, especially chapter 1
2. See the poetry of R.S. Thomas and a number of contemporary novelists, especially Iris Murdoch
3. See especially *The Sign of Jonas*, London, 1953
4. Alasdair MacIntyre, *After Virtue – a study in moral theory*, Duckworth, 1981
5. See Rowan Williams, *The Wound of Knowledge*, DLT, 1978
6. Williams, Op. Cit., p. 139ff
7. Simon Tugwell OP, *Ways of Imperfection*, DLT, 1984
8. Tugwell, Op. Cit., p. vii
9. Ibid., p. vii and passim

10. There are a number of people working in this "neo-aristotelian" industry, including G.E.M. Anscombe.
11. MacIntyre, Op. Cit., p. 2
12. Ibid., p. 11
13 Ibid., p. 30
14. Ibid., p. 51
15. Neitzsche saw this only too clearly. In this regard Carl Becker in *The Heavenly City of the Eighteenth Century Philosophers* (Yale 1932 and 1960), analyses very lucidly the emptiness of much of the Enlightenment. More recently this whole theme has been taken up by Bishop Lesslie Newbigin in two works which should prove critical for the Western churches, *The Other Side of 1984* (WCC, 1983) and *Foolishness to the Greeks*, (SPCK, 1986).

6

Where Could We Still Go Wrong?

One of the characteristics of Western men and women is a form of quiet cynicism. We do not wish to give credence to anyone else any longer. We have shut the door to those who would give us dreams of a better world, and are usually quite happy, even at times very determined, to dig our own back gardens. We have seen the rise and fall of too many heavenly cities for us to wish to build any more. Fanaticism of any kind is definitely a non-starter.

One might have thought that this insularity was a particularly English disease brought about by loss of empire and the apparent failure of post-war social optimism, but it is also a disease of each Western nation. It is often codified into political form by the New Right or into religious form by the Moral Majority, but it derives, essentially, from a form of quiet, despairing self-protectionism, a resignation. It is a belief, if it can be adorned with that word, that really nothing very much more can be done. All that can be done now is that people should cultivate their own situation. In this scheme of things religion is understood to be that which reinforces the sense of the individual's importance in the face of social and cosmic collapse. The Church is the last refuge for those suffering from anomie, and faith gives the individual hope in the face of darkness. Church study groups, when asked what signs of hope there are in the world, answer that there are none, apart, perhaps, from the odd place like Iona or Taizé, which the middle classes treat more as tourist attractions than as places for renewal.

This might not be the whole picture by any means, but it is certainly an important interpretative aspect of it. It confirms at the pastoral level the picture we painted in the last chapter, of the collapse of the framework of thought inspired by the eighteenth-century Enlightenment. One social historian writing as long ago as 1932 predicted this collapse. He saw that the dreams of the philosophers would only be replaced by further dreams and then further dreams still. He wondered whether the best attitude for people in the twentieth century might not be a quiet cynicism.[1] Effectively this is the situation we find ourselves in.

The difficulty is that cynicism, however quiet, does not pre-empt conflict. A retreat before the collapse of the social and moral order into personal and moral individualism does nothing to reduce the risk of conflict, it actually heightens it. Personal preferences become increasingly important, but there are no sure means of reconciling differences between these preferences when, in fact, they are nothing more than stated preferences. Conflict then becomes inevitable if people want to live together, which, in reality, they do. This risk of conflict is then extraordinarily heightened, intensified to an unbearable degree, by the growth of nuclear power and the use of high technology in communications and warfare. People's awareness of being on the brink of conflict in any case, derived, as we have said, from the loss of consensus over moral ends, is intensified to a terrifying level by their awareness of being on the brink of conflict in the nuclear age. The presence of the bomb, our knowledge that this would be the ultimate disaster, together with our knowledge that we are unable to solve even the smallest and most personal of conflicts very easily, is actually terrifying. Others have charted the course of this despair and terror. Our novelists and film makers are, in fact, far better at portraying the essence of our moral implosion than our theologians and philosophers, whose task, properly speaking, it ought to be. We are the hollow men, as T.S.Eliot said; and it was a very exact sense of understanding which inspired Francis Ford Coppola to portray Marlon Brando reading Eliot's poem of that name at the climax of his film about Viet Nam, *Apocalypse Now.*

Although few theologians have attempted the task it is possible to understand the growth of political cynicism in theological terms and to trace some of its impact upon the nature of believing in the twentieth century.[2] It is the pain, the actual deadening, horrifying pain of living in the modern world which is at the heart of things. Most of us totally underestimate the existence and importance of this pain as a factor in our lives. It is glossed consistently. But the pain forces us to disown responsibility, to say No to the task of confronting and assimilating the problems of modern existence. We have too much pain to be able to choose the good. The existence of this pain deadens and numbs our moral existence. Our reserves of compassion seep away, our desire for real living is undermined by the task of moving from one day to another with the minimum of disaster. There is a sickness of the spirit abroad which forces us into cheap or sentimental theological solutions. An avoidance of moral conflict, a ready acceptance of so-called religious experience, whatever its origin or quality, these are the signs of a cheapening of the religious spirit in men and women. This is the direct consequence of our inability to accept, assimilate and take into our active lives the pain of contemporary existence. And for those who profess to understand pain and who exalt the lordship of one who reigns from the cross, this is a double tragedy.

Moral cynicism compounded by terror has the effect of forcing the individual and the corporate state into a condition of paralysis and superficiality. There is too much loss. The condition of dislocation, of separation from the possibilities of true choice and self-confidence, is compounded and reinforced by continual exposure to hopelessness and terror. We look after what we know but this is a false peace, a superficial living, an acceptance of the immediate as true because we are terrified of the monsters that lurk in the deep. Those sea monsters have to be kept locked away, and we have to continue our voyage on the surface of the painted sea.

This is the social and psychological context of our contemporary exploring. Religious proposals, ways of seeing things, which do not take this context into account, which do not allow that the climate of despair and terror we have been describing is actually part of the inner make-up of the human personality in the Western world, and hence part of its theologizing, are hardly being perceptive about the condition of humanity. But most people reject this. They do not believe that religion really has anything to say to them in their present impasse. It is better to live, they might say, with the simple realities that one knows and recognizes rather than launch into grand solutions. Most people suspect that religion will only give you more trouble. Or they may say that the religious way is a form of opium or pixie dust. They either embrace it warmly precisely because it is that, or, for the same reasons, would rather do without it or choose their own forms of private comfort.

It is against this background that the religious philosophy of Don Cupitt has become important.[3] For Cupitt provides a religious, or at least apparently religious, way of coping with what is. People warm towards what he is saying because he confirms their scepticism as being correct and places it within what he would call the mainstream of Christian spirituality. He has understood the anomie, the emptiness and darkness of the modern experience, and is effectively saying to modern men and women, "Yes, what you are experiencing is within the gift of God, it is really a form of dark night of the soul, what you have to do is be courageous and stay within it." And he then points to a number of near contemporaries such as Kierkegaard, Wittgenstein, Albert Schweitzer and others, who had the courage to launch out alone and were, in the darkness, apostles of the new way. This vision is immensely compelling precisely because it understands the present interior condition of modern men and women, and encourages them to see that where they are is ultimately of God. It rejects the metaphysical stories of the past as just one more set of tranquillizers offered to the people by the officials of religion. This rejection gains its appeal from its tacit acceptance of the Marxist criticism of religion – and all of us have taken a great deal more of that criticism on board than we will admit – and its appeal to the modern sense of isolation and inner scepticism. It is a serious, in fact the most serious, contender for the position of Defender of the Faith for dislocated modern man. It is so precisely because it is a way of viewing things which accepts that modern men and women *are* dislocated beings. Cupitt's point is that this dislocation is not a terminal illness but in fact the beginnings of health. We have, he implies, been waiting for this moment for a long time, for what has caused man's illness is the imposition upon him of a supernatural metaphysic. Now he is at the point where he can begin to throw this off and stand on his own feet. This might well be a painful process but it is the only way. Man can now truly "come of age".

Cupitt's philosophy is also attractive because it incorporates the traditional "religious" values of gentleness and consideration for others. Indeed Cupitt insists that it is only when we have accepted our modern condition that truly disinterested love, what the New Testament calls *agape*, is possible. He sees his modern spirituality as a means, the only effective means in the modern climate, of being able to continue to practise the traditional virtues of disinterested love of neighbour, self-denial and detachment *for their own sakes*. This, Cupitt claims, is the way of transcendence, for it is within the quest of the individual, facing the darkness of the self, striving to live a life of virtue in a totally disinterested way, that the transcendence of traditional theism now resides. It cannot be doubted that there is more than just a tinge of Buddhism in this way, and this Cupitt gladly accepts, openly bringing the virtues of that austere faith (or at least its more austere, Hinayana, form) into clear conjunction with the Christian understanding of charity. There is an interesting passage towards the end of one of Cupitt's books where all of these themes are brought together, particularly the emphasis, which is Buddhist as well as Christian, upon death and the necessity for modern man to accept death as the means towards a true religious consciousness.

It is the fear of death, the fear of our own abandonment, loss and dissolution that creates the false, fearful craving ego at the root of our unhappiness. Those who have

died to death have attained the highest happiness and can
fulfil the moral requirement. . . . Objectifying faith is no
defence against death, for its objects do not, in fact, defend
us. It will have to be lost *then*, and if it will have to be lost
then, then for God's sake let us lose it now! So objectifying
belief in God is no defence against death, but to have a
divine consciousness is to have conquered the fear of
death . . . And what is the best way of learning this divine
consciousness? Strangely enough it is the discipline of
autonomy, for autonomy is disinterestedness . . .[4]

There can be little doubt that Cupitt's form of faithfulness for
those caught in the emptiness and dislocation of modern
existence is exceptionally attractive. It is attractive spiritually
because it accepts the spiritual condition within which
Western men and women find themselves, and it is attractive
intellectually because it is based upon a historical analysis of
the sources of our dislocation which would be widely
accepted, even by Cupitt's detractors. Like Alasdair
MacIntyre and Bishop Lesslie Newbigin, the heroes of our last
chapter, Cupitt accepts that the sources of our condition lie
within the rationalism of the eighteenth century. He accepts
that

some time around the year 1700 – give or take a generation
either way – a disastrous split took place. The leading edge
of European spiritual development broke away from Christianity, and the gap has been slowly widening ever since.[5]

Cupitt's point is that this is not a disaster but actually something to be accepted and from which a new form of "faith" can
emerge. This he calls "hyperborean faith".

Hyperborean faith represents an attempt to live a free
and truthful Christian life, without nostalgia, illusion or
the traditional insatiable hunger for power over others,
in the world as it now is.[6]

Later on he explicitly contrasts his own view with that of
Alasdair MacIntyre. He says that MacIntyre is unable to
prove his point, implying that his exposition is a sort of
whistling in the wind, hoping for the return of a moral
universe when we are faced with daily evidence of its
dissolution. Cupitt would ask that we allow ourselves to be
swept on by the course of history and allow the dissolution
of the structures to take place, for this is the only condition
which also allows for or facilitates the uprooting of
egoism. We have to pass through this fire.

It is at this point that we should begin to wonder. The
argument has seemed terribly plausible and attractive up
until now, but is there such a real and necessary contrast
between egoism and a true religious faith? Does faith
actually lead to the total denial of the self? Is our
twentieth-century condition, with its moral indifference
and terror, really such a fertile seedbed for religious consciousness? Is there not also a sense in which we have
reached a curiously negative and empty condition, a condition of moral implosion which is corrosive of *any* sort of
faith, hyperborean or not? Certainly, for most ordinary
people, moral or religious stances of any kind are extremely difficult if not impossible. Nobody wants to take
them on board. The possibility of "hyperborean" faith
becoming a reality amongst the vast majority of people
appears, at first sight at least, to be remote and something
of a fantasy. People in Western society are more puzzled
and confused, caught in the regular processes of daily

living, fearful of unemployment, death or penury. Our capacity to make individual moral choices has been seriously undermined by war and terror. Certainly our confidence has been seriously shattered even if we still feel that the religious and moral guidelines are reasonably intact. Moreover, many would say that individual courage to live without illusion is in fact an extremely expensive luxury, available perhaps within well protected academic milieux, but in the end incomprehensible to those who face a daily struggle to avoid tragedy with some degree of cheerfulness. And so whereas Cupitt's approach to Christianity appears to accept the modern condition, it seriously underestimates its depth and the desperation with which most people live. To then say that in order to be religious you have to accept this desperation comes across as unreal, and verges on being another tyranny, a form of cultured despising of the depth of tragedy and suffering men and women face.

This sort of criticism might give the impression of being easily made, but it can be put in more philosophical terms.[7] Don Cupitt is, of course, quite right to demand that God should be God, and that men and women should have faith *because* God is God, and not because such faith provides them with some form of felt protection against evil, some insurance against destruction, or some confirmation that they are "all right", when in fact they are supporting or conniving at a social fabric which causes destruction or oppression. This much we do know. But human beings need more than this, and although our need of a thing is by no means proof of the existence of that thing, if religion is always purely disinterested, what Cupitt calls "an assertion of the naked will against what is the case", a number of different things will begin to happen which, when carefully examined, are, religiously speaking, undesirable.

105

In the first place, such a quest for disinterestedness will dissociate the practice of religion from the human emotions. When the emotions and the quest for virtue are disallowed, then the will is enthroned as central in the human psyche. This is really very misleading as a means to understanding how human beings act. Actions do not simply arise clear and fresh from the spring of the human will. Their source is far deeper and far more unclear. The fact that Don Cupitt admits to placing the philosophy of voluntarism at the centre of this scheme of things already places him on the side of those theologians of the Middle Ages who may well have brought about our dilemma. He has effectively decided, without a lot of argumentation to prove his case at this point, that modern man is unable to reach back into the deeper sources of human action and so, like it or not, has become a voluntarist. We must accept that this is the case and live with the dislocation that the twentieth century gives us. This is hardly credible, especially when we see around us the damage that has been done to people and societies by the obsessive desire to act and choose rather than to attend. Simone Weil makes the point when she says

We have to try to cure our faults by attention and not by will.[8]

But this is not the only difficulty. We do, as we have already seen, actually need the inspiration of beauty and goodness. We can only function as human beings when praise and gratitude, celebration, delight and desire are part of our religious practice. This is where we can turn once again to the vision of the English devotional writer who most clearly understands the importance of these

human emotions in the religious life – Thomas Traherne.
Cupitt emphasizes disinterestedness. He claims that disinterestedness is the only real way to God in the twentieth
century. Desire for God and delight in his beauty are
suspect, they lead us into a form of faith which posits God
as real, for there must be a real object of our desire and a
real God in whom to delight. But real descriptions of God
cannot do anything, Cupitt claims, except lead us into a
repetition of the old metaphysics, a repetition of the old
theological imperialisms from which we are now, in this
century, just beginning to set ourselves free. Traherne's
vision challenges all this. He, like Bernard of Clairvaux in
an earlier more monastic context, does not avoid the religious importance of "desire" for God and delight in
God's creation. He urges us to capitalize on our sense of
desire if we are to be led into the knowledge of God.
Disinterestedness is a sign of unbelief. Desire, or
"wanting" as Traherne calls it, has actually been given to
us by God in order for us to desire him who desires us.
"Wanting", or longing for God, is not "pixie dust" but
essential to faith. It is pagans who do without it.

> It is very strange; want itself is a treasure in Heaven: and
> so great an one that without it there could be no
> treasure. God did infinitely for us, when He made us to
> want like Gods, that like Gods we might be satisfied.
> The heathen Deities wanted nothing, and were therefore
> unhappy, for they had no being. But the Lord God of
> Israel, the Living and True God, was from all eternity,
> and from all eternity wanted like a God. He wanted the
> communication of His divine essence, and persons to
> enjoy it . . .[9]

Cupitt would object that this ascription of "wanting" to God actually undermines God's freedom. He cannot be really free if he has to "want" something. And it must be admitted that this emphasis on the freedom of God has been a very important part of contemporary theological exploration. Traherne, on the other hand, points out that the freedom of God — so important to those who stand in a fiercely independent protestant position — is not affected by his "wanting". God's desiring does not diminish him, he embraces it freely. So, by correspondence, should we, if we are to discover our status as sons and daughters of the most high.

The risk of Traherne and those who favour a more "realist" approach to religious practice and experience, is that God will become so real as to be oppressive, so "objective" as to become tyrannical, so much "the object of our wanting" that we cannot discover who we are to want him. This is, of course, the "fault" in religion so accurately pinpointed by Karl Marx. "Wanting" will, he says, inevitably lead to our own alienation and an alliance between the forces of oppression and religion. We must keep ourselves free. Marx's argument would be fatal if it could be shown that when religious people understand God in an "objective" way this *always* leads to some form of alienation. That it can and does should not be doubted. That it does so inevitably is not true. Belief in an objective God is not necessarily alienating. Marx asserted that those who live by grace regard themselves as dependent. But not all dependence is a source of alienation, nor is all "grace" the source of oppression and corruption.[10]

This is crucial because it gives us pause and turns us back to a form of religious practice which acknowledges a pressing need to purify itself of its alienating power (and who does not know something of that?), but refuses to accept that all dependent relationships, all acts of graciousness from one source of being, human or divine, to another, automatically and necessarily carry that seed of oppression within them. We can then affirm the possibility of a religious practice which is neither so full of oppressive objectification that it becomes the tool of an oppressive society, nor so pure and "disinterested" that it cannot express the desire for and delight in the other that the human psyche needs for its own freedom. It is this combination that Cupitt appears to regard as impossible. Delight in the other and human freedom are not so far apart from each other as either Marx or Cupitt would appear to suggest.

So the historical development of religious consciousness in the West actually leaves us in a very vulnerable position. We risk, according to Marx and Cupitt, practising a form of religion which is full of objective truths, none of which, according to Cupitt, are provable in the present climate, and all of which, according to Marx, are the tools by which hierarchical societies keep themselves hierarchically structured. If we abandon these objective truths then we will fall into an experiential religion which, in the end, is a form of emotional purgation and which is just as much a form of social reinforcement as the doctrinal and objective religion which it replaced. The grave risk is that because they are aware of the difficulties of an experiential faith, Westernized men and women will do no more than baptize the pain and anomie of being Western, and simply endure in a kind of stoic individualism whatever it is that the politicians and the world of work can throw at them.

Don Cupitt is the symbol of this stoicism. It is actually far more widespread in practice than we realize. Most people probably adopt a form of it in order to exist, and many formal religious believers probably practise this form of faith with a fair degree of consciousness. What Don Cupitt has done is to give it a certain degree of religious and intellectual credibility by drawing on Buddhism and St John of the Cross in its exposition. The important point about this form of religious practice is that it affirms very strongly the principle of "detachment" in the spiritual life. Detachment from the illusory requirements of the self is a primary goal of the religious life, and in so far as such a stoicism as we have been describing encourages that, it is to be welcomed. After all, detachment is not obviously a primary feature of Western religion. But that said, such a religious stoicism really entails a serious category mistake about the nature of religion.

It makes the mistake of assuming that we can cope with what is and talk about that coping in religious terminology, and assume that this is "believing". Such a form of faith appears to provide the Western individual with a religion, when in actual fact it is only an affirmation of his already existing way of life using "religious" terminology. It is a form of baptism of what civilization has made of us. Moreover, because of its emphasis upon the primacy of the will in the very act of "coping", this way separates the will from love, desire and delight. Religion then becomes a matter of the will, using as a definition of the will one which by Christian standards is very defective. Love, desire and delight in turn become very personal matters, tacitly excluded from the realm of religion. Once this division occurs then the contemplative approach to religion is lost. The contemplative approach[11] seeks to bring the human person together again in a movement of love, desire and delight — "wanting", to use Traherne's language. This unites the will with love, the intellect with wisdom, and action with adoration.

If in the face of all this the Western stoic Buddhist intellectual objects that he is being led back into an acceptance of the existence of a transcendental being, who is the object of this movement of love, desire and delight, then there is a simple enough answer. And that is this. The praying person actually needs to know that when he prays, with love, desire and delight, there is a being who is the object of his longing. He needs to know this not just for his personal satisfaction, nor simply to give him hope that his prayers may be answered, but *for the sake of the integrity of his act.* We do actually need to know that our prayers are more than the action of spiritually autonomous individuals doing what spiritually autonomous individuals have to do. If there is no way of telling that our prayer is any more than a disinterested action, then our prayers actually fall into disrepute, for they are then reduced to being no more than a means of personal fulfilment. At this point in the game people will recognize that there are other, more evidently effective, means of acquiring fulfilment than those provided by the disinterested religious path, especially if that religious path is the Christian one with its emphasis on sacrificial sanctity, and they will certainly pursue them.

And so we are left once again with the original insights of Traherne. A movement of the soul in delight and desire towards God in creation is the movement for which we were actually created. It will unite our dislocated being, but it will also take us away from that most serious of contemporary dangers, quiet cynicism. It will restore our joy. Moreover, in the face of our pain, and contemporary pain is real and will remain real, integrity is recovered, not by abandonment to what is, but by an actual movement towards goodness, with all the laughter that such a movement brings. This is a movement for hope, for life, for a new creation, for the human being who, in truth, lies hidden, fearful, in the midst of our interior sense of disaster. It is also the movement, within us, of God.

I must lead you out of this into another world, to learn your wants. For till you find them you will never be happy: wants themselves being sacred occasions and means of felicity.[12]

You must want like a God that you may be satisfied like God.[13]

Be sensible of your wants that you may be sensible of your treasures. . . . What you wanted from all eternity, be sensible of to all eternity. Let your wants be present from everlasting. Is not this a strange life to which I call you? Wherein you are to be present with things that were before the world was made? And at once present even like God with infinite wants and infinite treasures: Be present with your want of a Deity, and you shall be present with the Deity. You shall adore and admire him, enjoy and prize him; believe in him and delight in him, see him to be the fountain of all your joys, and the head of all your treasures.[14]

Notes

1. Carl Becker, *The Heavenly City of the Eighteenth Century Philosophers*, Yale, 1932
2. See Rowan Williams, *The Truce of God*, Fount, 1983
3. Don Cupitt is a prolific author, but see especially *Taking Leave of God*, SCM, 1980
4. Cupitt, Op. Cit., p. 161
5. Ibid., p. 155
6. Don Cupitt, *The World to Come*, SCM, 1982, p. 6
7. I am greatly indebted, at this point in the argument, to an important article by Rowan Williams – "On Not Quite Agreeing with Don Cupitt" – which appeared in *Modern Theology*, Vol. 1, No.1
8. Simone Weil, *Gravity and Grace*, p. 105
9. Thomas Traherne, *Centuries of Meditations*, 1.41
10. See Nicholas Lash, *A Matter of Hope*, DLT, 1981, p. 182
11. See Thomas Merton, *Contemplation in a World of Action*
12. Traherne, *Centuries*, 1.43
13. Ibid., 1.44
14. Ibid., 1.45

7

Attention

One of the themes running right through Thomas Traherne's *Centuries of Meditations* is an emphasis on seeing things right, or rather, seeing things as they are. What things are is glorious. Things are shot through with the divine life. Human beings are sons and daughters of the Most High, princes and princesses, kings and queens even, of the Kingdom. For various reasons men and women are unable to see this. We are unable to see things as they really are before God, and unable to see ourselves or the creation properly. We are prevented from so doing by sin. We are dull and blind. We need, he says, "open eyes". When our eyes are open we are able to see how we and the creation are "in God".

This capacity for true sight or discernment is for Traherne, not simply a quirk, a trick of the mind or the eye, something we can do if we practise hard enough. It is wrapped up in the use of intelligence, the practice of love and the development of the virtues. It is not something which is exercised apart from those other qualities. Seeing things as being "in God" and not at the same time being drawn to love, wonder and the exercise of goodness is an impossibility. He makes this clear at one point by saying,

I saw moreover that it did not so much concern us what objects were before us, as with what eyes we beheld them, with what affections we esteemed them, and what

114

apprehensions we had about them. All men see the same objects but do not equally understand them. . . .[1]

He goes on to talk about the human faculties of knowledge, life and love. These faculties, he says, require the objects of creation in order to come to fruition. He remembers Aristotle's famous epigram "Felicity is the perfect exercise of perfect virtue in a perfect life", and concludes the paragraph by saying

> For that life is perfect when it is perfectly extended to all objects, and perfectly sees them and perfectly loves them: which is done by a perfect exercise of virtue about them.[2]

Traherne understands, as almost no other English devotional writer or theologian except perhaps Julian of Norwich, that "All things are in God eternal". What is needed is to turn and see, not just with the eyes, but also with the heart and mind, that this is the case. Happiness then floods the soul.

This is not a new theme. It is present in the Revelations of Julian of Norwich.[3] It is also present in other religious paths.[4] It is, however, a difficult path for us to tread because daily living in Western society has become so extremely fragile and superficial. We are intent on seeing what we want for ourselves rather than looking at things as they really are. We have allowed our sight to be dictated by our apparent needs, and so live not just on the surface of things but also, in some real way, apart from things as they are. Our capacity to see is diverted. We are dominated by the false self which seeks pleasure or activity as good for its own ego. We have become dangerously out of touch with things as they really are – which is only another way of saying that we have become deeply unspiritual beings.

Perhaps it would help if we tried to clarify what is meant by the word "spiritual". The word "spiritual" as used in the Christian tradition should have two particular implications, whatever else it is used to mean. First, it should imply that there is a single reality. There is not a worldly realm and then a completely separate spiritual realm. Second, it should lead to the realization that human beings tend, inherently almost, to live simply on the surface of this reality, living with an understanding of it which they wish to present to others or which they can accept for themselves. Most of what they are is ignored. To be a spiritual being, therefore, is not to abandon this world in favour of another, supposedly more real, more spiritual world; it is to live with what has been given to us. It is also to live with what has been given to us in its deepest possible dimensions. It is to live from deep within what we truly are, and to know that what we truly are springs from God. This is the teaching of Thomas Merton when he says,

> The only true joy on earth is to escape from the prison of our own false self, and enter by love into union with the Life who dwells and sings within every creature and in the core of our own souls.[5]

To be spiritual is to delight in all that one is and in all that one has been given. If this is what it means to be spiritual then the spirituality of Western society lies within the finitude of that society, within what it is and what it does, within the finitude of its work, within its daily living – provided that this living is conducted at the deepest possible level. It means "seeing" all that is, including the self, as being ". . . in God eternal".

116

But Western men and women have become dislocated people who live on the surface of things. We are aware, certainly, that there are powers unknown, lurking beneath the surface of our lives; but we are somehow unwilling or unable to allow ourselves to be in touch with these deeper powers. In the end we sail on the surface of the sea – and it is, after all, a very pleasant sea on which to sail. We visit island after island and tell each other all about each of the islands we have visited, but are not easily satisfied and are, therefore, basically unhappy. This dislocation between our surface existence and our inner being has materialism as its symptom. The quest for more things, more distractions, more "capital", is the symptom of our inner dislocation. Materialism is not simply having things or owning things, it is a condition of the mind or spirit whereby the person attaches himself to things, money, status, job, rights even, in order to be assured of his identity. Materialism itself is not the disease. Nor will our disease be cured merely by having or owning less. Materialism is a symptom, a symptom of an inner dislocation which causes us to concentrate upon "having" or "owning" as a remedy. The Buddha would have called it "attachment". This "attachment" is a sign of our inner dislocation, which itself prevents us from being in touch with the true sources of right action in the world.

This inner dislocation has been commented upon by spiritual writers for a very long time. It seems to become particularly acute at times of great social change. The Dutch priest, Henri Nouwen, comments upon it. He calls it "loneliness", but it is quite evident from his description of the disease that he means far more than mere isolation. He describes our often amusing attempts to escape from this loneliness, and offers this very funny quotation from Henry David Thoreau:

When our life ceases to be inward and private, conversation degenerates into mere gossip. We rarely meet a man who can tell us any news which he has not read in a newspaper or been told by his neighbour; and for the most part, the only difference between us and our fellow is that he has seen the newspaper, or been out to tea, and we have not. In proportion as our inward life fails, we go more consistently and desperately to the Post Office. You may depend upon it, that the poor fellow who walks away with the greatest number of letters, proud of his extensive correspondence, has not heard from himself this long while.[6]

This dislocation between the surface self, sailing on the painted sea, and the inner self, lost in the murky depths, is well known to the American contemplative monk, Thomas Merton. As we have seen, Merton talks about the "false self" which is really the result of illusion and self-deception, and contrasts this with the "true self", which is the abode of Christ. He says,

Social life, so-called "worldly life", in its own way promotes this illusory and narcissistic existence to the very limit. The curious state of alienation and confusion of man in modern society is perhaps more *bearable* because it is lived in common, with a multitude of distractions and escapes – and also with opportunities for fruitful action and genuine Christian self-forgetfulness. But underlying all life is the ground of doubt and self-questioning which sooner or later must bring us face to face with the ultimate meaning of life.[7]

Much Western civilization derives its obsessive drive from a form of corporate dislocation, or, as others have it, alienation. Our obsession with successful economics, our obsession with political theories which will work, all of these derive from our dislocation. The real questions are "How does this dislocation occur?", and "How can it be remedied?" We act superficially, we are caught within a network of superficial activity, and we know that we need to bring our actions out of a deeper well, a deeper inner integrity. We want to know how this can be the case. In the first place we want to know this for our own sakes; we want to lead integrated, happy lives. We also want to know for the sake of those towards whom we act. Those towards whom we act will be harmed unless our action springs from the integration of our actions with the ultimate sources of life. They will be harmed if our action is an obsessive one derived from the desperate hunt to cover our dislocation by answering our felt needs. Such a desperate hunt ends in the manipulation of people and circumstances in accord with these felt needs alone.

So the problem of "right action" is a very real and a very deep one for contemporary men and women. It involves the question of personal happiness. At another level it involves the question of identity and of personal security in that identity. Once we know who we are within ourselves, and know that more confidently, then we shall know how to act. Being and action will then be linked together in a continuity of secure identity. Knowing how to act cannot be reduced to working out the right answers from some tablet of stone given to us by somebody else. The most unhappy feature of Western society is that we are always looking for a tablet of stone; indeed, we spend a great deal of time looking at a whole series of tablets of stone presented to us by a succession of distinguished people, and call this deep capacity for indecision a happy freedom of individual choice. Once we are secure within ourselves then we will be happy to listen and choose. We will be content both with our own choices and with those made by others which may affect us adversely. Thomas Merton puts this clearly.

> To have identity is not merely to have a face and a name, a recognizable physical presence. Identity in this deep sense is something that one must create for himself by choices that are significant and that require a courageous commitment in the face of anguish and risk. This means much more than having an address and a name in the telephone book. It means having a belief one stands by; it means having certain definite ways of responding to life, of meeting its demands, of loving other people, and in the last analysis of serving God. In this sense, identity is one's witness to truth in one's life.[8]

So the problem of right action is in reality the problem of who we are. What principles I seek to act upon, and how I choose these principles and allow them to bear upon what I do, is intimately bound up with who I am, with who I am before God and with what sort of God I am before. Action and belief are part of the same bundle of things.

We must therefore take responsible human action more seriously and understand it at a deeper level. Human action, in order to be fully religious, needs to be more surely in touch with its roots. We desperately need to get off the painted sea of life. In order to do this our understanding of action needs to accept some basic and necessary shifts in orientation. These shifts are basically three:

1. *From* seeing action as having its source and spring in the human will,

    to seeing action as the human person's response in freedom to the goodness of his own self and the total goodness of creation.

2. *From* seeing action as individually owned, leading to ideas of individual rights as paramount, and because individually owned therefore easily threatened by other powers,

    to seeing action as an "acknowledged" response to God's love springing within and fed by prayer and deep adoration.

3. *From* a view of action as somehow good in itself and necessary to us if we are to remain human beings (i.e. I act, therefore I am),

    to a view of action as something for which we may well be responsible but which is primarily something for which we have to wait.

All this might be summarized by saying that we need, at the root of our being, a basic shift of orientation *from action to attention*. This shift of understanding, so vital if we are to retain our fullness as human beings, will not come about easily; perhaps it will only come about as the result of suffering. Yet while it may at first sight seem to be very alien and actually very difficult to make and sustain, in actual fact it is not so very far from any of us. It is a shift of orientation which lies just below the surface, waiting, as it were, for us to acknowledge and accept it. Once acknowledged and accepted it becomes a true source of liberation and dignity. It also enables us to exist with a great deal more happiness and good humour than most Westerners manage at the moment.

That such a shift of emphasis is really not so very far away has been understood by the novelist and philosopher, Iris Murdoch. Her novels illustrate, often comically, the effects of people trying to live by means of the rational will but being far more swayed by other forces which, foolishly, they cannot await. In her philosophical writing Iris Murdoch spends a long time setting out an alternative view to the one which dominates much contemporary philosophy and literature. This "way of seeing" is then incorporated, embodied as it were, in her novels. The contemporary view she decries might be called, somewhat scathingly, the "action man" view. It is the "action man" who identifies himself with his will and whose will consists in choosing. Anything else this man may do is a shadow life. This view Murdoch finds alien and intolerable on philosophical as well as on moral grounds.[9] She is opposed to the prevailing contemporary view that man is essentially a willing, acting, public person, and argues very powerfully in a completely different direction. She points to the ways in which human beings actually deepen their moral appreciation and understanding of each other. Individuals are known and knowable by love, not simply by observation, decision and action. If we are to be fully human beings, and able to act as such, then we need more than "willing" or "choosing"; we need the concept of "attention". The word "attention", which derives initially from the work of the French existentialist writer, Simone Weil,[10] expresses the idea of a just and loving gaze directed upon an individual reality. The point that Iris Murdoch makes is that this goes on all the time, not just at the point of action or decision, and builds up within us a picture of what the world is really like. In the end it is in accord with this "inner" view that we will act. It will, at times of crisis, burst out upon us, sometimes with comic as well as passionate results. This view makes for slower progress and slower achievement in persons, but in the end the person will be "truer" if he or she can discover what it is that is being built up within them. It also means that the celebrated condition known as "existential angst" is put in a lesser place and not allowed to dominate human behaviour. What does dominate us is

... a patient loving regard directed upon a person, a thing or a situation. . . .[11]

It is, therefore, that which goes on in between human decisions which is more important than the decisions themselves and the so-called rational processes by which we make those decisions. It is how we form ourselves, or allow ourselves to be formed, that matters, so that when decisions come they are made in obedience to who we really are and how we understand things.

There is, therefore, considerable agreement between Iris Murdoch as a philosopher criticizing the prevailing philosophical tradition of our day, and people like Thomas Merton and Henri Nouwen, who are set within the mainstream of Christian spirituality. The analysis is broadly similar on both fronts, stressing the importance of establishing personal moral integrity — ourselves as moral agents — and abandoning the apparently free but in reality false self floating on the painted ocean of civilization. These words put the case very clearly (they read as if they come from Thomas Merton but are actually from Iris Murdoch):

As moral agents we have to try to see justly, to overcome prejudice, to avoid temptation, to control and curb imagination, to direct reflection. . . . Man is not a combination of an impersonal, rational thinker and an impersonal will. He is a unified being who sees and who desires in accord with what he sees.[12]

Iris Murdoch then takes the argument a stage further. She broaches the whole question of moral improvement. Given that we are, at root, moral agents, concerned to discern and attend to moral ends, can we actually make ourselves morally better? Goodness is a difficult ideal, but, she says, it ought to be the philosophical ideal. Philosophers have spent far too much time talking about what is right, they should now turn and ask themselves "What is good?" What is good and how can we become good? She suggests, simply, that the answer is to be found in prayer. Prayer, for her, is attention.

 Prayer is properly not petition but simply an attention to God which is a form of love . . .[13]

What she says is that if our behaviour is to be reoriented, to take us into goodness, then we need a very profound reorientation, a different source of energy for the person which comes from elsewhere, from a different source. There are obstacles to this. Human beings, for example, form attachments and these easily become obsessive, and when they do they produce bad action and need to be displaced.

 Our ability to act well, when the time comes, depends partly, perhaps largely, upon the quality of our habitual objects of attention . . .[14]

The enemy of right action is fantasy, personal fantasy,

> . . the tissue of self-aggrandizing and consoling wishes and dreams which prevents one from seeing what is outside one.[15]

We need to be set free from this fantasy world if we are to act truly. In order to do that we have to practise true *detachment*. If we pay attention to great art or beauty, then we shall learn, slowly, how things can be looked at without being seized and used, without being drawn into our greedy selves. Contemplation of nature by the naturalist exhibits this quality. Beauty attracts unselfish attention. We must learn to direct our attention outward, away from the self which grasps and reduces. Here is a longer passage which clearly summarizes what she is saying.

> It is in the capacity to love, that is to see, that the liberation of the soul from fantasy consists. The freedom which is a proper human goal is the freedom from fantasy, that is the realism of compassion. What I have called fantasy, the proliferation of blinding self-centred aims and images, is itself a powerful system of energy, and most of what is often called *will* or *willing* belongs to this system. What counteracts the system is attention to reality inspired by, consisting of, love. In the case of art and nature such attention is immediately rewarded by the enjoyment of beauty. In the case of morality, although there are sometimes rewards, the idea of reward is out of place. Freedom is not strictly the exercise of the will but rather the experience of accurate vision which, when this becomes appropriate, occasions action. It is what lies behind and in actions and prompts

them that is important, and it is this area which should be purified.[16]

Such a passage only serves to show how close Iris Murdoch is to the central Christian tradition concerning the need for grace and redemption. Her emphases on the necessity to free the soul from attachments could be paralleled many times, especially in the writings of the Desert Fathers. The important conclusion is that she, together with a number of others, is pointing a way to understanding and then to binding up some of the dislocations suffered by modern men and women. They have seen something of the dangers we face in our modern age, and are reaching back into an earlier tradition for the sources of unity and healing. They are also, more importantly, reaching back behind the superficiality of a willed or rational response to our difficulties, recognizing that our current emphasis upon what we can *do*, so enthroning the will as central, is no more than a repetition of the problem. We need a more effective answer. So Merton and Murdoch concur. We have false selves or a false understanding of the roots of action by the self and need to return to our true end. Attention to our true end will give us inner security and identity, even though this final "end" is beyond us. We have, for too long, considered that action is ours.

Notes

1. Thomas Traherne, *Centuries*, 3.68
2. Traherne, Op. Cit., 3.68
3. Julian of Norwich, *A Revelation of Love*, especially Chapter 5

4. See especially the delightful book about Buddhism by Anthony Harvey, *A Journey in Ladakh*, Fontana, 1984 (incidentally, it is dedicated to Iris Murdoch!)

5. Thomas Merton, *Seeds of Contemplation*, Anthony Clarke Books, 1972, p. 20

6. Henri Nouwen, *Reaching Out*, Collins, 1976, p. 30

7. Thomas Merton, *Contemplative Prayer*, Darton, Longman and Todd, 1973, p. 26

8. Thomas Merton, *Contemplation in a World of Action*, George Allen and Unwin, 1971, p. 59

9. Iris Murdoch, *The Sovereignty of Good*, Routledge and Kegan Paul, 1970, p. 9

10. Simone Weil, *Gravity and Grace*

11. Murdoch, Op. Cit., p. 40

12. Ibid., p. 40

13. Ibid., p. 55

14. Ibid., p. 56

15. Ibid., p. 59

16. Ibid., p. 66

8

Wisdom

We have talked at some length about how those of us who live in Western society tend to live very superficially. We separate our surface existence from our depths and live only with the former, flitting from one activity to another. It is important, we said, to wait and to attend rather than to act.

A very similiar pattern emerges if instead of looking at how we act we look at how we come to *know*. All of us depend a very great deal on knowing. We live in societies which have made heavy investments in education and the pursuit of knowledge. Most of us have deliberately chosen to share in this investment and, in one way or another, will encourage our children to do the same. Formal education for the first twenty years or so of a person's life has an enormous effect, and there is little sign that we will change our minds about the importance of doing things in this way. Nor can there be any doubt that the investment we have made in education has made an enormous difference. Things happen which men only dreamed of a hundred years ago. People live – in vast numbers – who previously would have died. Understanding and delight occurs where otherwise there would have been pain and suffering on an enormous scale. Major diseases have been eradicated from vast areas of the earth's surface. Hunger and the fear of malnutrition have been forgotten by whole sections of the human race. And yet, as we have seen, we are still puzzled at what we have done. We are unhappy, unless we are very unfeeling, at the effects of this long investment in the pursuit of knowledge, unsure whether it has actually solved the problems of living. Knowing more does not seem to make us a lot better. It certainly does not enable us to share the fruits of the earth more fairly. If anything, to the ordinary man, it seems to make the problem worse. Knowing is a sort of complication, a sort of disease which gives you more problems than you had when you started out and meanwhile prevents you from getting on with the ordinary, practical affairs of everyday life in an effective way.

That certainly is a very popular view, although probably not one on which to base much social policy. It might be better to have a careful look at what is happening within some of our educational establishments rather than simply succumbing to such fashionable anti-intellectualist criticism. What is happening is quite different, disturbing certainly, but in a very different way. It is disturbing for the establishments themselves, but more so for us all, because schools and universities are really very clear models of what is happening in society at large. They are places where so many of the dreams and desires which we have about ourselves are actually worked out in practice. What happens there illustrates profoundly what is happening to all of us.

The most important thing that is happening is that people are ignoring the hidden side of their existence. Any educational institution has a double agenda. The first, the obvious and overt agenda, what one might call the public agenda, concerns teaching and research. It concerns the quest for and the exposition of the truth about such diverse matters as the life of Mozart, the development of fibroid cysts or the behaviour of atomic particles. The second, hidden, agenda concerns choices and values. Who will teach about Mozart or fibroid cysts or the behaviour of atomic particles? How much will be spent on these matters? Who will receive what will be spent and how will the spending be assessed? – these are all questions which will have to be decided on this agenda. The answers to these questions are usually fairly overt, what is hidden is the process by which the answers are obtained.

What goes into that process is a number of factors whose importance cannot be underestimated but which are usually unspoken because unspeakable. These are such things as the values people live by; the fears, both real and imagined, which people suffer from; the ambitions, both realized and abandoned, which inhabit the human soul. These hidden factors are, in reality, far more influential and far more important than the primary agenda of teaching and research which a school or a university sets for itself. Usually the hidden agenda governs the public agenda to a considerable degree. This is frequently recognized, but not many educational establishments have developed mechanisms whereby those who work in them can talk about the importance of the hidden agenda and its nature except in bars or in bed. Most people are busy saying that they are asking academic questions when they know that the questions themselves, as well as the answers, are being determined by an enormous hidden activity. Perhaps this is why novels about the academic life hold such a fascination. They contain a great deal about the hidden agenda of academic life and provide, like most novels, a means of self-understanding and analysis which is not public and consequently not a threat. This is further evidence of a distinct dislocation between the public and the private which requires comment but which cannot be commented upon except in literary terms.

Examples of how this happens are not difficult to find. There is the case of the Lecturer in mid-career. He is now forty and has a family of three children and an intelligent wife who is increasingly – and rightly – bored by life at home. He may or may not have been made Senior Lecturer by now. If he has then he can take some consolation in his security of tenure in the present climate, but if he has not then he has little to compensate him for the increasing dullness of his existence, the ever increasing administrative load, and the impossibility of moving to a more creative and stimulating department in another university, where the Head of Department would not be so scathing of his undoubted achievement. Earlier in his career he enjoyed teaching, but now he feels he has heard all of the comments that any student can actually make and has provided all of the answers too many times over. He cannot move. He is too bored to write. His wife sees him as somewhat washed up and uncaring, selfish even, in his preoccupation with his lost career. His students see him as waspish and distant, clever, perhaps, but not much of a friend.

Then there is the Professor who has set up an international study unit in his particular field. He has spent a great deal of time travelling the world in search of funds and delivering himself of the latest fruits of his research in conference papers. He is, in many ways, successful. But his University finds him difficult to talk to, his staff quarrel amongst themselves about priorities, and his wife has left him. His mistress is very attached to him but she is aware that her existence in his life is somehow no more than an adjunct for her partner's quest for recognition. Who he really is has not been revealed, either to her or to himself.

In each of these examples, neither of them really very far from reality,[1] there exists in a person the same disjointedness which we have seen can exist at the level of policy formation. This dislocation is the bread and butter of those who are professional counsellors to students or educational institutions. So many of them find the same thing in different forms. Put simply it is that thinking and intellectual activity are being divorced from feeling and caring. Emotional development does not command the same parity of esteem in tertiary education as mental development. This dislocation then actually inevitably affects the type and style of intellectual enquiry that goes on.

What we are really doing is asking the question "what is knowing all about?" Part of the answer can be found within the judaeo-christian tradition. It does not take a great deal of biblical exposition to show that in the Hebrew Bible the verb "to know" has a far wider and richer set of meanings than it does in modern English. It is used to denote sexual union in the famous phrase, "Adam knew Eve, his wife" (Genesis 4 and passim in the Old Testament). It is associated with silence in "Be still and know . . ." (Psalm 46 and Ruth 3:18), and it is often the heart which is regarded as the seat of knowledge [cf. Jeremiah 24) when "the heart" is also the seat and centre of the personality as a whole. A frequent use of "know" in the Old Testament is in the phrase "know that I am the Lord", where knowing obviously includes faith, allegiance and the acceptance of a mutual relationship.

This tradition is continued in the New Testament, where St Paul incorporates knowing into loving and where knowledge is derived from or at least involved in acts of faith and love. A particular instance can be found in the letter to the Philippians which reads,

My prayer is that your love for each other may increase more and more and never stop improving your knowledge and deepening your perception so that you can always recognize what is best. (Jerusalem Bible translation)[2]

Our modern view would find this sequence of love leading to the improvement of knowledge and discernment very difficult to follow. We normally regard love as being either in some strange way something which follows upon knowledge, saying that we will be able to love more if we know more; or as being a passion which sweeps all knowledge along in its path. We find an intrinsic connection between the two difficult to maintain. Paul sees love as a richer and less heady affair, something which when alive actually enables knowledge to occur.

For a long time the Christian tradition maintained the priority of love and faith over knowledge, or at least refused to separate knowledge from love in any clear way. This fusion was maintained at least until the end of the Middle Ages. Anselm asserted the ancient sequence in his phrase *fides quaerens intellectum*, and indeed his *Proslogion* is an extended meditation on the way in which love leads to knowledge. St Thomas Aquinas, who has come to be regarded by many as the high priest of intellectualism, is in fact, as a number of modern scholars have pointed out,[3] not very far from this tradition. He owes a great deal more to the classical monastic tradition than we have realized. It was he who, in the end, turned to silence as the most complete expression of his apprehension of the divine.

But this is to progress too quickly. What is this "classical monastic tradition"? It is, put simply, the view that learning only properly occurs within a fully moral life where prayer and a corporate attempt to be free from the illusions and fantasies that the self is heir to are regarded as intrinsic to the learning process. Such a life is exemplified by the monastic existence at its best. Knowledge, when all is said and done, is knowledge of God, and God himself is the teacher. This tradition is not the same as medieval scholasticism, even though many of the medieval scholastics were monks or the products of the monastic life. Popular views of the monastic life of the Middle Ages often assume that all monks were scholastics (and scholasticism is usually understood to be just an older version of that modern scourge, "intellectualism") or vice versa. That they were not and that the monastic tradition struggled, vainly, to preserve its life against the increasing strength of scholasticism in medieval Europe, is one of the fruits of the work of a contemporary monk, Jean Leclercq. His beautiful study of monastic culture chronicles the differences as well as the links between the monks and the scholastics. He contrasts the monastic life, as exemplified by Bernard of Clairvaux, with the urban scholastic schools and their mentor Peter Lombard. "Monastic" theology may well have used, from time to time, the methods of the schoolmen with their study of the Trivium and Quadrivium, the seven liberal arts, but at the end of the day the monks were not liberals, acquiring knowledge by means of the *quaestio*, but radicals, living before God alone within the liturgical framework of the monastic life and under the guidance of a spiritual father. This is a more contemplative tradition where, says Leclercq,

The important word is no longer *quaeritur* but *desideratur*, no longer *sciendum* but *experiendum*.[4]

St Bernard's exposition of "knowing" is entirely in line with the sequence laid down in the sentence from Paul's letter to the Philippians. He says,

> It is not disputation, it is sanctity which comprehends if the incomprehensible can, after a certain fashion, be understood at all. And what is this fashion? If you are a saint you have already understood, you know; if you are not, become one and you will learn through your own experience.[5]

Before this begins to sound too mystical it should be understood that St Bernard and the monks are as much concerned with consent to God as with the knowledge of God. They understand "knowing" as something which involves consent to what is and so co-operation with what is, a participation in God's action in and through the existing world. A certain amount of this "monastic" theology derives, of course, from a protest against the worldliness of scholastic knowledge and how it might lead to titles and honours which would provide ecclesiastical or civil preferment. Richard Rolle, the English mystical writer, was certainly involved in this protest. But it is also an assertion of what knowledge really is and how it may be obtained. An epistemological assertion is at its root. For the monk knowledge of a kind may be gained by rational processes, but the fullness of knowledge, which will include the rational, derives from within love and the school for love which the monastic community must be.

An important implication of this "monastic" view of knowledge is that it involves the whole self. The monastic criticism of the scholastic view was that their quest only involved a part of the self, namely, the rational. Monastic knowledge came about within a community of love. This means that in the monastic view there cannot really be any such thing as *my* knowledge. There is knowledge, certainly, but strictly speaking this is God's knowledge of the world and of me, and I may share in it. Knowledge as possession or property, or even as achievement, is therefore quite alien to this tradition.

There is a sense in which this kind of knowledge might be better described as a pain, or at least as our response to pain, namely the pain of loving which impresses itself upon a human being. It is, strictly speaking, more an expression of loss rather than gain. Something of this is expressed in a quotation from Jerome which Bernard often used,

The work of the monk is to weep, not to teach.[6]

Apparently Aquinas makes a similar point in his exposition of the Beatitude "Blessed are those who mourn" (Matthew 5:4). His view is that this Beatitude is especially appropriate for those who seek knowledge. This is because all learning makes an impression upon the mind which the learner experiences as painful. In this sense learning is a passion, a suffering, and we can only learn as much as we have suffered.

The quest for knowledge, therefore, must be recognized as something which exists at the deepest levels of the human person. It involves his original state and so cannot be satisfied merely by the exercise of curiosity. Once the quest for knowledge is severed from this original state, by appropriating it to the intellect alone, then the quest will never end, or will always end in temporary and fleeting conclusions. The monastics of the Middle Ages, Bernard and Thomas Aquinas in particular, understood this very clearly, and were deeply afraid that the scholastic approach, far from being a means of achievement, which it claimed to be, was in fact a form of resistance, a building of barriers, a local and temporary staunching of the bleeding of true knowledge. The quest for knowledge, they were saying, becomes superficial when we refuse the passion. We must allow knowledge to derive from and to remain within our yearning, our mourning for the lost element within ourselves, our longing for God. The implications of this for the contemporary academic community should not be difficult to see. In spite of the claims of modern academics to belong to an international community, it is obvious to many who live and work within that community that it is anything but a community of love, and that progress within it depends entirely upon accepting a view of knowledge as a commodity which can be owned or acquired by the individual. This simply accepts our contemporary dislocation as inevitable and even right.

Meanwhile it is worth remembering that a number of contemporary voices are picking up the monastic refrain. One of them, the Welsh priest-poet, R. S. Thomas, encapsulates the monastic view in his poem "Roger Bacon" which contains the lines:

> Yet
> he dreamed on in curves
> and equations
> with the smell of saltpetre
> in his nostrils, and saw the hole
> in God's side that is the wound
> of knowledge and
> thrust his hand in it and believed.[7]

Another is, of course, Thomas Merton. He contrasts knowledge with wisdom.

> Actually, our whole life is a mystery of which very little comes to our conscious understanding. But when we accept only what we can consciously rationalize, our whole life is actually reduced to the most pitiful limitations, though we may think quite otherwise.[8]

Merton also has an essay on the nature of university life in which he consciously recalls the contemporary American university to its monastic roots. He asserts that the function of a university is to help the student to discover himself, to recognize himself and to identify who it is that chooses. He readily admits that such a definition is "monastic", and that for him the university and the monastery should have the same function. What has happened, however, is that universities have abandoned their true function in favour of a

> superficial freedom to wander aimlessly here and there, to taste this and that, to make a choice of "distractions" (Pascal) which is simply a sham. This claims to be a freedom of "choice" when it has evaded the basic task of discovering who it is that chooses.[9]

In talking about the rival mediaeval traditions of university and monastery he claims that the aim of both of them was the activation or "ignition" of the inmost centre of the human person, the spark of the soul which is a "freedom beyond freedom". This the modern university conspicuously fails to do. It concentrates upon the falsity of success when the important thing is to learn the value of unsuccess. He comments somewhat sharply on his experience in a modern university.

> The danger of education, I have found, is that it so easily confuses means with ends. Worse than that, it quite easily forgets both and devotes itself merely to the mass production of uneducated graduates – people literally unfit for anything except to take part in an elaborate and completely artificial charade which they and their contemporaries have conspired to call "life".[10]

This is sharply put, but R. S. Thomas and Thomas Merton are among those who have understood how in the Western world the human psyche has been dislocated, and are attempting to provide means whereby one aspect of this dislocation, namely the split between the life of the intellect and the life of love might be bound up together. A dislocation between the life of the intellect and the life of love carries great risks. At the social level the risk we take is that under the influence of such a dichotomy universities and academic institutions will actually cease to function as places for the interchange of knowledge. Knowledge which is restricted to the discoveries of the individual intellect is invariably restricted to those who understand the "language" within which that particular knowledge is enclosed. Modern universities generate "languages" or "codes" for the transmission of information which, in the end, only a very few people can understand. These "codes" are sometimes incomprehensible even within the broad spectrum of a single discipline, let alone across the university community itself, and very few universities or polytechnics actually encourage or enable their members to spend time listening to or learning the language of others.

Meanwhile the unlettered outsiders are seldom the bene-
ficiaries.

For knowing to be transmuted into "knowledge" in the
fullest sense academics need to be academics at a spiritual
level. The academic profession is, if the argument we have
followed is in any way correct, a spiritual profession, heir
to the monastic rather than the scholastic tradition, and
one which must be pursued at the most profound level of
the human personality and with all the grace and wit and
heart of which human beings are capable. If it is not
pursued in this way then it falls into idolatry more quickly
and more surely than almost any other profession. In the
end the academic profession is a profession of love – believers would say of the love of God – hidden by, or
disguised as, the pursuit of knowledge. To ignore that
means that academic institutions will quickly and surely
fall into heartlessness.

At this point it might well be objected that such a
"monastic" view of knowledge is contrary to received
wisdom. Surely, it will be said, knowing is of value in itself,
and surely our progress as people has depended on our
acceptance of a value-free understanding of knowledge. In
particular this view underlies scientific progress. Without it
science could not progress. How can the scientific community possibly allow the intrusion of values into the
scientific quest, when it has been repeatedly shown that it
is only when this community pursues its task without
reference to political or moral values that progress can
occur? Are we to return to the monastic superstition of the
Middle Ages when the Enlightenment has set us free? This
will only be the thin end of a wedge, at the thick end of
which lie political controls of the worst sort. Our progress
and happiness depend, it will be objected, upon the

140

academic community being left to pursue the truth without constraint and to enjoy research, if necessary, simply for its own sake.

Unfortunately this view is being criticized by the philosophers of science themselves. It is increasingly seen to be a view which only disguises a great deal of value-laden inquiry which is being carried out by the scientific community without those values being examined or discussed or even tested in any way. This avoids the basic requirements of empiricism which the scientific community has set itself to uphold.[12] The scientific presupposition is that the pursuit of knowledge is good in itself. A fatal flaw in this presupposition is that science has failed to relieve our social ills which, it must be conceded, are still enormous. The scientific community will then respond that the pursuit of objective truth must not be confused with the aim of meeting human need, indeed human needs can only be properly met when the truth is pursued objectively. This is really a profoundly irrational stance. It is irrational because it fails to adhere to the requirements of rational inquiry into the problems of living. This irrationality is exposed by one such philosopher of science, Nicolas Maxwell, when he reformulates the goals of science into a philosophy of wisdom. He says that the current emphasis upon a "philosophy of knowledge" is not really rational.

It is just these elementary requirements for rationality that inquiry pursued in accordance with the philosophy of knowledge violates. Far from intellectual priority being given to the tasks of articulating problems of living, proposing and criticizing possible solutions . . . it is all the other way round: problems of knowledge and technology are tackled in a way that is intellectually dissociated from problems of living, the latter, indeed, being excluded from the intellectual domain of inquiry altogether.[13]

Maxwell goes on to propose that the scientific quest will be better pursued and more completely fulfilled *as scientific quest* once the philosophy of knowledge (i.e. standard empiricism) is replaced with a philosophy of wisdom. In this "philosophy of wisdom" an approach to science which makes no judgement as to the value or usefulness of research (which inevitably leads to much trivia being produced) is replaced by an approach which involves both the heart and the head. Rational co-operation will replace individual élitist achievement, and vision will replace mere curiosity. The driving force must not be the acquisition of knowledge but a desire to understand the natural world and the place of mankind within it.

> In order fully to develop and make available the intellectual riches inherent in diverse aspects of science and scholarship it is essential to put the philosophy of wisdom into practice . . . inquiry pursued for its own sake is, at its best, an aspect of love, our shared endeavour to see, to apprehend that which deserves love, in the world and in ourselves.[14]

Maxwell goes on to argue that this is true even for such an "abstract" subject as theoretical physics. The division between the personal and the intellectual ought not to be allowed even here if the subject itself is to flourish. Scientists, claims Maxwell, are "lovers of the universe" and need to bring together their concern for objective truth and their own instinctive feelings and imaginings, and only when this occurs will there be any guarantee that a fully rational inquiry can occur.

So if we have not been convinced by Thomas Merton or Jean Leclercq that there is a dichotomy between knowledge and wisdom, perhaps we will allow contemporary philosophers of science like Nicholas Maxwell to convince us that in order for the Western preoccupation with "rationality" to flourish it needs to be reshaped by an understanding of "wisdom". Unless that happens the current ascendancy of the scientific enterprise will simply leave us with as many problems to solve, if not more and greater, than we had at the beginning of the century. In present conditions the purpose of a university, or any other educational establishment come to that, is to acquire and transmit knowledge; but knowledge is neither properly acquired nor properly transmitted if "knowledge" is all that is pursued. If people in the Western world are to be seekers after knowledge then they need to recognize that knowledge is not restricted to the discoveries of the intellect. If we do not do this then the knowledge of the Western world will become, if it has not already, a commodity to be bought and sold in the so-called free market economy. This will have the further consequence of subordinating the pursuit of knowledge to political processes. Nobody would claim that there must not be some degree of correspondence between the pursuit of knowledge and these processes – indeed there can hardly be anything else, but the pursuit of knowledge cannot be entirely subordinate to these processes, nor will it be if it remains true knowledge or "wisdom". The argument of this chapter is that the current subservience of the pursuit of knowledge to economic and political processes is the result of the acceptance by those living in the Western world of a reductionist understanding of the knowledge they pursue. If knowledge is something which I can acquire rather than a wisdom which I share, then knowledge becomes subject to political pressures, and people begin to ask how this knowledge can be acquired and how much they will have to pay to acquire it. At this point the politico-industrial machine moves in. Where a simple and univocal understanding of knowing prevails then we become one-dimensional people. Knowledge is a form of wound which must be allowed to bleed. Its purpose in bleeding is to feed the hearts and minds and souls of human beings in society. Universities, polytechnics, schools are, therefore, society's necessary wounds. The tragedy is that we feel that bleeding of this kind is somehow a waste of resources, and so attempt to bind everything into saleable and acceptable packages which will be useful to somebody, preferably the person with the most money. Those who need to benefit, the poor of the land and the hungry of the world, cannot do so. The result is dislocation and conflict.

After all this time it will come as no surprise to learn that Thomas Traherne has a lot to say about wisdom, and the need to move from the pursuit of knowledge to the development of personal wisdom, in his *Centuries*. In the third *Century* he reflects upon his time at university and how it enabled him to see "that there were things in this world of which I never dreamed". Study in itself is ultimately the study of God, which is why studying for self-ostentation or for the acquisition of power is to fall drastically short of the inner purpose which the pursuit of knowledge carries within it.

He that studies polity, men and manners, merely that he may know how to behave himself, and get honour in this world, has not that delight in his studies as he that contemplates these things that he might see the ways of God among them, and walk in communion with Him.[15]

He that knows the secrets of nature with Albertus Magnus, or the motions of the heavens with Galileo, or the cosmography of the moon with Hevelius – or of whatever else with the greatest artist; he is nothing if he knows them merely for talk or idle speculation, or transient or external use. But he that knows them for value, and knows them his own shall profit infinitely.[16]

So that to study objects for ostentation, vain knowledge or curiosity is fruitless impertinence, tho' God himself and Angels be the object. But to study that which will oblige us to love him, and feed us with nobility and goodness toward men, that is blessed. And so it is to study that which will lead us to the Temple of Wisdom . . .[17]

Notes

1. Brian Thorne "Can a University Care?" A talk given to the University of Bristol, 1983, *Areopagus*, No. 13
2. Philippians 1:9, Jerusalem Bible translation
3. Rowan Williams, *The Wound of Knowledge*, Darton, Longman and Todd, 1978, p. 125
4. Jean Leclercq OSB, *The Love of Learning and the Desire for God – A Study of Monastic Culture*, SPCK, 1978, p. 7
5. Cited by Leclercq, p. 137
6. Ditto, p. 256
7. R. S. Thomas, *Frequencies*, Macmillan, 1978, p. 40

8. Thomas Merton, *Seeds of Contemplation*, p. 105
9. Thomas Merton, *Love and Living*, Sheldon Press
10. Ibid.
11. See especially Michael Stancliffe, *The Falling Tower*, The University of Southampton, 1971. Stancliffe suggests that all academics should take time off regularly to write poetry! His work is much under the influence of George Steiner, who should also be consulted on this theme.
12. For an extensive and powerful treatment of this whole area see Nicholas Maxwell, *From Knowledge to Wisdom — A Revolution in the Aims of Science*, Blackwell, 1984
13. Maxwell, Op. Cit., p. 48
14. Ibid, p. 6
15. Traherne, *Centuries*, 3.41
16. Traherne, Op. Cit., 3.41
17. Traherne, Ibid., 3.40

9

Prayer

Prayer too is a form of bleeding, a wound which we may not staunch. Its source is in the incompleteness of the human person and its continuance depends upon that incompleteness, that wounding, being maintained. To be a prayerful and spiritual person requires an affirmation and an acceptance of one's incompleteness. It requires a realization that the important thing about human beings is their incompleteness. Human beings are characterized by the unstaunched wounds within their nature. They reveal these wounds by being those who continually and consistently look towards the future, always seeking a new heaven and a new earth, always hoping, always moving forwards. Doing this is what makes us human. To settle into a final completeness of understanding is to accept an ideology. To believe that you have found a complete explanation, a way of seeing things that explains and welds into a complete pattern all of the inconsistencies of life, this is to lock oneself into a diminishment of the human person. To believe that you have finally uncovered and understood the means of human fulfilment is to embrace the roots of fascism. We are all radically incomplete, wounded at the centre. The Christian Gospel is that which asks us to accept that incompleteness and to accept it as being, in itself, good news. Prayer then becomes that outpouring of the self which radically maintains and affirms our incompleteness, springing as it does out of our longing and desire. Prayer keeps us incomplete and to remain incomplete is the fulfilment of mankind.

All of this is, of course, in direct contrast to an understanding of prayer which sees its source as residing in the human will. Prayer seen as deriving from an act of the will must be the most discouraging way of understanding the whole process; discouraging because prayer will only then occur when something is wanted, and we know there are many things we want which we cannot or even should not have. It is also a limitation in the sense that the objects of prayer will then be limited to those things which we can envisage as being "good" for ourselves or for others. Furthermore such an understanding of prayer actually limits God to being a "willing" deity, a god whose primary reason for existence is to choose to grant or refuse the petitions of his subjects. All of this diminishes both God and man. Above all, such an understanding of prayer – placing its origins within the willing, rational life of human beings – only reveals exactly how far the contemporary process of dislocation has gone. It has reached right into the very bones and sinews of religious practice and persuaded us that even prayer must be regarded as a partial activity, something that we can do and which will, if we do it properly, produce results, and above all results which we can see. So prayer is reduced to being a product, something which we can make or do, another thing we can have if we are to be the properly fulfilled people we think we should be.

Prayer as property is no joke. Two recent articles in a popular magazine illustrate this. The first was a pull-out supplement entitled "How to Improve your Health". This contained check lists on diet and exercise and then one on "spiritual health". The necessity of regular prayer was added to the list of exercise, yoghurt and a regular consumption of dietary fibre. Not that either prayer or dietary fibre are bad in themselves. They simply do not belong to the same class of things. The same magazine carried an article about a "spiritual marriage". This described a couple who, after some years of matrimony, had decided to abandon sex and live on muesli and yogic exercises. They clearly felt that they had everything they wanted except some form of spiritual fulfilment, and had now decided to obtain that as well. Their mistake was to assume that spiritual fulfilment was something which could be "obtained" by behaving in particular ways. Prayer and the spiritual life have become items on the consumerist shopping list; they have become totally absorbed into an individualistic consumerist materialism, reduced to another acquisition of the "fulfilled" person. To associate prayer or spirituality with fulfilment is to make a category mistake of the first order. Prayer is not fulfilling in that sense; if it is it is not prayer.

Prayer is a dark struggle, a struggle with the angel who then leaves us with a permanent limp, a dislocated joint. Prayer is a radical refusal to accept that I can be completed by the conditions prevailing in Western society. Praying is a radically subversive act of protest against all self-contained and totalitarian understandings of mankind of whatever kind, including the theological ones. All prayer is a protest against the inevitability of determinisms, a protest against the idea that there is no alternative.

Prayer, moreover, is an affirmation and acceptance of the unknowability of God. God cannot be seen. This is the fundamental truth of religion. It is a truth usually ignored by contemporary evangelical religious movements, who while they would deny having seen God immediately give the lie to this statement by replacing the darkness of trust with the certainty of assured "knowledge". The statement "God cannot be seen" does not just say something about sight, it also says something about incomprehensibility and about the basic necessity of trust. The statement "God cannot be seen" is not merely a truth of a somewhat unpalatable nature, to be accepted with regret as if it should not be so, rather it must be embraced as life-giving, or at least understood as life-giving once embraced. God cannot be seen, he can only be trusted. Gregory of Nyssa spoke of this when he said that on Mount Sinai Moses only saw the "back-parts" of God. And the theme has been taken up in our own day by the Welsh priest-poet R. S. Thomas. In the poem "Pilgrimages" he writes:

> . . . He is such a fast
> God, always before us and
> leaving as we arrive. [1]

Prayer as an affirmation and acceptance of God's unknowability is beautifully expressed in the poem "The Presence".

> I pray and incur
> silence. Some take that silence
> for refusal.
> I feel the power
> that, invisible, catches me
> by the sleeve, nudging. . . . [2]

Prayer then is, or should be, an act which is content to rest in the silence of God and to accept that this is, although painful, ultimately good. This prayer is a radical protest against final descriptions of God, against "knowing" in a debased sense. It is, therefore, a radically subversive act of protest against theology as description, against doctrine simply as a series of true and rational propositions, against those who imply that they have "seen" God or the inner metaphysics of Jesus Christ. It is interesting that Gregory of Nyssa also makes this point when he suggests that to be content with the "face" of God is to be content with less than what God is. If you have seen God you will not pray.

Furthermore we will not understand prayer until we see religion as lying at the root of all human affairs. Prayer then involves all things, and is an attempt to bring all things into focus, to see all things as they really are, as seen by God. It is not a religious act which will somehow alter the way things are, it is rather an expression of faith in the godwardness of all things and an attempt to align oneself with that godwardness. A religious view of life is not strange, it is life seen as it really is.

It might help our understanding of matters at this point if we were to look again at our use of the word "spiritual". As we have already recognized, the word "spiritual" should imply two things in particular – that there is a single reality and that human beings must not live on the surface of this reality. Perhaps, for the time being at least, we should lay aside the word "spiritual" itself. Its dualist connotations obscure the affirmation of the unitary nature of reality which it contains. Perhaps we should replace it with the word "hidden". Spiritual realities are in fact hidden realities, things which, for various reasons, we cannot see at the moment. To be a spiritual person is to be someone who sees things as they really are, who sees things from the inside, whose vision is not clouded by fantasy or illusion. To be spiritual is not to be ethereal but to be perceptive of hidden truth, obscured or forgotten agendas. It is to be aware of deceit and "covering", the self-protection in which the soul engages, and to bring those hidden or forgotten truths gently into the light.

Sometimes indeed these forgotten truths will be of a very material kind. They may be truths which require action of a direct or immediate nature. To see them and to do them is to be a spiritual being. This, in the end, is something of the burden of St John's Gospel. The truth, the Word or Logos, is there, but men have missed his coming. We can, by attention to and faith in the existence of the hidden Word of God, see him, but when we see the truth it has to be done in order for us to become part of it.

This is why the word "spiritual" and the reality of what it means to be spiritual has to be placed firmly within the arena of public life and not secreted away into a separate existence known as "religious". One important reason for this is because so much of our public life, our public discussion of politics and economics, is conducted in a totally superficial manner. But the superficiality derives not so much from the lack-lustre arguments but from a lack of comprehension as to why people come to understand and accept truth in the first place. The sterility of public debate is a sign of our dislocation. We assume that people primarily exist in an intellectual or rational mould. We are nervous of linking a person's intellectual convictions with his inner orientation as a person, with his hiddenness or his spirituality. That, we assume, is his private affair, and his mental activity can quite easily dissociate him from all that.

Once again we are thereby caught in a particular kind of sterility because of our refusal or inability to recognize the place that the spiritual plays in the intellectual and moral development of the person. We have become so dislocated that we are unable to see the hidden bleeding that is going on within the person or group of persons with whom we are faced. And yet we do know, instinctively almost, when certain arguments are being proposed which function within the life of the proposer as more than just arguments. We know when these arguments are part of the given reality for that person and constitute a whole way of seeing things. We also know that in order to persuade the same person that his or her way of seeing things is false or misleading, simple rational argument will not prevail, however rational or accurate the argumentation may be. The position of the proponent derives from certain experiences, and reflections upon these experiences which have then become locked into a certain understanding of life. These experiences have become the interpretative experiences for that person by which everything which comes his way is judged. In the debate about nuclear weapons, for example, the traumatic experience of Europe at war and the events leading up to that war have, for many people, become determinative in the whole discussion of the nature of defence.

The only thing which will affect a change of position is a further set of interpretative experiences more powerful than the first. Not to see this and allow for it as we discuss nuclear weapons is to betray just how dislocated we are. Prayer and spirituality then become important as those realities which enable people to remain open to change and development, maturation of various kinds. They are also those realities which enable people to discern between false and unnecessary change and real, needful change. Without prayer we should simply be open to the force of the strongest set of experiences and be forced to accept those as determinative. Without prayer we are crippled, living either by a single immutable set of interpretative experiences, unwilling or unable to change, locked into nostalgia maybe, or a monistic world view which may or may not correspond to reality; or we are subject to the whims of fancy, fashion and the strongest life force around, unable to decide which of the experiences we have are to be accepted as interpretative for us.

Genuine spirituality is that attitude of heart, mind and will which prevents me from doing one of two things. It prevents me from allowing a particular set of powerful interpretative experiences from becoming so important that they become an ideology, so predetermining all rational response. It is also that which prevents me from so not knowing which of several conflicting sets of powerful interpretative experiences are "mine" that I am tossed from one set of views to another, and so live continually at the mercy of the strongest set of forces available. Either way lies dislocation from my true self and the true ends of that self. Prayer keeps me in touch with myself, it prevents me from so damming up the life of grace that I staunch the bleeding of the spirit within me. This is where the old theological concept of grace is still relevant. Grace, the free gift of God's love, enables me to trust gladly in the partial nature of human insight. It prevents me from putting my complete trust in a single set of experiences which then become ideological and so exercise a dehumanizing impact upon me. Grace prevents me from putting my trust in princes rather than the invisible and unseen God. It is that which enables me to trust that new and equally genuine and formative experiences may be in store for me – that God has new truths waiting to break forth from his word – and, just as important, that I will be able to discern which of these truths is from God and which is the product of illusion or fantasy. Grace enables me to trust myself to the processes of change both in me and in society, and so liberates me to participate in the creation of a new world with confidence. To do that is to believe in God.

But unfortunately it is not quite as simple as that. While we might recognize that prayer is necessary to our health as human beings, we do not recognize quite so easily how prayer is used to reinforce or protect who or what we are and what we possess. Prayer itself may become part of our dislocation, and instead of allowing us to bleed healthily may be used to stop the bleeding and to shore up a particular way of life. At a particular point religion, and the spiritual practices which accompany it, becomes oppressive, a duty rather than a source of liberation. At a particular point human beings take their religious selves so seriously that their spirituality becomes a "structure" or "sacred canopy",[3] an "act" which they adopt because they feel they ought or because they need the protection they believe it brings or because they are, quite simply, afraid.

There is an inbuilt tendency in humanity to turn religion into a structured possession in order to reinforce their position in society, or to protect them from their own inadequacy or to preserve their own power. The roots of this kind of "structuralism" are fear and desire. The use of religion as an unconscious front for inner fear and confusion is often present in closely knit religious communities. This is difficult enough, but the more difficult situations are to be found where religion is overtly used as a supporting mechanism for power. This happens blatantly in South Africa and Israel as well as, latterly, in America and Northern Ireland. It also happens within the recesses of our own souls.

It is well known that some of the most savage attacks

upon religion as a prop for power and capital come from the pen of Karl Marx. A contemporary philosopher who, in a study of the relationship between Christianity and Marxism, has understood most clearly how religion functions as an ideology, is Denys Turner. Ideology, he says, is

a socially lived falsehood.[4]

Religiously speaking, it is contained in the relationship which obtains between the authoritarian preacher declaring from his authoritarian pulpit that the people of God are all equal, and the reciprocal acceptance of this act by the people themselves. Both the preacher and his congregation

socially live an enacted contradiction, a contradiction which is internal to their form of life.[5]

Turner goes on to unravel the ways in which prayer can also participate in this "performative contradiction" which is characteristic of ideology. The Marxist can only too easily conclude that Christians are

fated, by the demands of their own discourse, to live out a permanently uncertain and ambiguous relation with the demands of the material social world.[6]

Turner does not think, however, that Christianity is *inherently* ideological; rather he thinks that the supreme contribution which Marxism can make to Christianity is to rescue it from the permanent necessity of being ideological. He does see certain forms of Christianity as ideological, for example, some specific forms of twentieth-century Christianity which are rooted in Barthian "fideism". These forms of faith seem to reply on no evidence whatsoever, and so cannot be contradicted by any evidence whatsoever. When this happens

> religious language is . . . materially one of the ways there are for not knowing the social forces which govern our material world; it is a way of living out a contradictory relationship with reality.[7]

What is particularly interesting about what Turner is saying – at least for our present purposes – is that it reveals just how little Christians realize that their activity participates in a condition of "not-knowing". He lends considerable philosophical support to the popular notion that religion in general and Christianity in particular participate in and lend reinforcement to the ideological condition of modern man. In this condition men and women are forced to live "out of joint", living a contradiction between their true series and the selves with which they are provided by the social forces of the age. Thus ideology and dislocation become one and the same thing.

On the purely practical and observable level the churches do use religion as a means of accruing to themselves at least the sensation of power if not actual power itself. It should disturb us greatly that religion becomes a matter of big business, with spiritual fulfilment being sold in churches which claim success in evangelism. We should be even more disturbed when we realize that many of these churches are set in urban areas where the divide between the rich and the poor is as great as it ever was, if not greater, and in a nation where the resources available for the deprived are being cut back day by day. This "ideological" condition of the churches is especially visible in the large conurbations of the tropical third world. The churches of the third world often claim to have large congregations in the cities, together with a considerable development of "spiritual" awareness and thousands being added to their number each month, yet this happens with very little regard – except amongst a small number – for the living conditions of the many thousands in favelas and townships of the worst kind in their immediate vicinity. Never has Denys Turner's "performative contradiction" been more evident as far as Christianity is concerned. Nor is this simply a third world problem. It happens in the West and it happens to us individually.

All of this can only mean that much religion has become a means of protection *against* seeing. The more religious we are, often the more blind we are. Religion then becomes a source of alienation rather than of peace and freedom. Religion and oppression, historically at least, have a strange fascination for each other, and those who claim to be religious without actually recognizing that this is true can hardly substantiate the claim. The further difficulty lies in persuading people that this is so. Persuading people that they risk being the victims of a "performative contradiction" when they go to church is not an easy task. We are conditioned into believing that if a person prays or goes to church then that is automatically and necessarily a good thing. As most good pastors know, nothing could be further from the truth; but there is no rational process which will enable us to understand that this is so. Such a condition is the result of our dislocation. Religion, in the Western understanding, is seen to be adherence to a set of beliefs which are understood by the believer to be "true". This effectively relieves him of the task of seeing himself and his beliefs within their social context. We are the victims of adherence to the tenets of religion rather than the existence of the living God. Perhaps we should read Meister Eckhart (or his contemporary champion, Don Cupitt) when he says,

> Anyone who looks for God in any particular way gets the way and lets go of God.[8]

Human beings cannot deliver themselves of the need to pray, and indeed prayer does liberate from ideology; but, strangely enough, prayer and worship can also be the sources of the deepest alienation known to man, especially when these religious practices become allied to power, and so effectively support the structures of oppression. Prayer can either release us from dislocation or it can be used to reinforce it.

But this set of insights into the contradictory nature of prayer is by no means new. In particular they were known to those who began the monastic tradition in Christianity by fleeing to the Egyptian desert in the fourth century. The remarkable thing is that these Desert Fathers fled to the desert at the same time that Christianity became the established cultus of the Roman Empire. They sought for a true spirituality because religion was becoming a source of alienation, reinforcing the oppressive structure of the state. But they also knew that the problems of men were at root spiritual ones, and so they went to the root of their lives to rest in the silence of God. They sought salvation and the avoidance of sin, and by sin they meant the contradictions of a dislocated existence. They sought to avoid alienation, whether this was economic, political or religious. They knew that the problem was finally an inner one, deriving from interior restlessness. Cassian reminded his monks that even the desire to save others could derive from a restless inability to sit still and accept oneself. The task of the monk was to come face to face with God, and to avoid all the disguises which life and religion allow us to wear and which prevent that eventual encounter. As Thomas Merton was aware,

> Once spiritual experience becomes objectified it turns into an idol. It becomes a thing, a reality we serve. We are not created for the service of any thing, but for the service of God alone, who is not and cannot be a thing.[9]

The inner purpose of the Christian faith, that is, not why we must have faith, but what it must do to me if I have it, is to enable me to abandon my disguises, to take me out of my divided and dislocated self, and to give me a face, the face which God gave me at the beginning.

> "When you said, 'Seek my face', my heart said to you, 'Your face, Lord, I will seek'. Do not hide your face from me . . ."[10]

The face we really have, the one with which we shall be able to see "the goodness of the Lord in the land of the living", the face with which we see God and which he sees in us, this face is present and may be discovered in us in silence, peacefulness and solitude. Solitude is essential to sight. Silence is essential to speech, and prayer is essential as the place where, if we persist long enough, disguises will drop away. We have to lose these disguises, which in the end are only expressions of our dislocation, if we are to live with God and our fellow human beings as a human being.

To pray is to descend with the mind in the heart and there to stand before the face of the Lord, ever present, all seeing, within you.[11]

Notes

1 R. S. Thomas, *Frequencies*, Macmillan, 1978, p. 5
2 R. S. Thomas, *Between Here and Now*, Macmillan, 1981, p. 107
3 See Peter L. Berger, *The Social Reality of Religion*, Penguin, 1973, especially chapter 1
4 Denys Turner, *Marxism and Christianity*, Blackwell, 1983, p. 6
5 Turner, Op. Cit., p. 31
6 Ibid., p. 172
7 Ibid., p. 172
8 Cited by Don Cupitt
9 Thomas Merton, "The Inner Experience", an unpublished manuscript cited by William H. Shannon, *Thomas Merton's Dark Path*, Farrar, Straus, Giroux, 1981, p. 129
10 Psalm 27:8, 9
11 Theophan the Recluse cited in *The Art of Prayer*, p. 63

10

The Good Life Regained

If then, we are to "stand with the mind in the heart", as we are before God, and so recover our sense of delight, we will need to move from a way of viewing things which relies upon the primacy of the rational, willing, independent self to a style of life which revolves around attention, wisdom and contemplation. This way is traditionally known as the "monastic" way of seeing things, but only in the sense that the monastic way is a symbol or focus for the rest of us. It is not a way which is restricted to those who have taken monastic vows. It is open to all. We might well call it an "interior" monasticism.[1]

There are a number of features in this way of life which it is worth emphasizing. It is a way which will bring us into very close contact and even comradeship with others who intrinsically rely upon "attention", on waiting and upon wisdom rather than knowledge, even though our philosophical presuppositions may not be the same as theirs. These include not only the poets of the Western world but also the prophets amongst us, those who can see that by a reliance upon these older "monastic" virtues we will actually disrupt the established order in those places where the quest for knowledge alone has removed us from our true selves. We will be brought into an alliance with those who delight in the earth and wish to preserve within it a way of behaving — rather than simply a way of thinking — which is related to our true ends as human beings and the goodness which it is ours to glimpse and release amongst us. This will mean, I believe, taking far more seriously than most Western Christians do at the moment, the strong European tradition of Marxist humanism, and bringing that tradition into closer contact with the monastic thread in Christianity. It was this task which Thomas Merton attempted, and perhaps failed, to do in his last years. We will, thereby, inevitably be involved in action to re-order our social existence, actions to re-establish the place of equality, the sharing of talents, full regard for the powerless and unlettered, and to redevelop those skills of hand and eye which our mind-based society has neglected.

How all this can be achieved will continue to be a matter for sharp debate. Can it actually happen without violence? Are the mythologies which imprison us too strong to break otherwise? And Christians will make their contribution to this debate – as they are doing in South Africa – without fear and always looking to the crucified one. But this creative re-ordering will always be with people, not for them. If it is not with them in the first place then it will never be for them at the end. This programme will also involve us in taking solitude and silence far more seriously than most Westernized individuals are able to do. Solitude and silence, engaged in positively, are purgative. They enable us to drop the illusions we create in self-protection, and at least provide the environment within which we may discover our true selves and the awkward, uncomfortable but in the end liberating truth about ourselves. We need to be more silent with each other than we normally manage, if only so that the quality of the re-ordering we are engaged upon should be what it needs to be rather than what we, in our fevered state, often perceive it to be.

This shift will also involve us in some theological re-orientation. We desperately need a revival of a spirituality of delight, and have in these pages tried to outline at least the basic elements of such a way of seeing things. Among them can be found a radical acceptance of the basic and original goodness of all that is. Also needed is a recognition of the centrality of forgiveness and compassion for the self and all that is, a forgiveness which is actively expressed and which when followed involves us in the re-ordering of existence which compassion requires. Another element is such trust in the basic and original goodness of things that we are led into a ready acceptance of loss, a "letting go and letting-be". This requires a recognition that the existence of pain is not, in itself, an evil. Refusal to countenance pain leads to more evil than pain itself contains. All of these elements find their source in delight; delight in the self and in the creation, delight in the awkward beauty of what is given rather than the culturally generated beauty which enslaves the Western consciousness.

All of these features stand in marked contrast to a way of seeing things which is based upon the priority of redemption from sin. A fall/redemption-centred spirituality has dominated the Western Church since Augustine and is the theological reverse side of the philosophical coin which dominates the Western way of life. In this tradition original sin and redemption play a central role, together with a number of associated concepts, especially justification by faith alone, a substitutionary theory of the atonement and an extreme emphasis upon "power" in the work of God and the Holy Spirit. This way of seeing things is not only closely linked to a rationalist philosophy, it also produces ways of personal behaviour and forms of social philosophy which rely upon "control" rather than discipline, upon a bleak self-denial in the spiritual life and upon hierarchical and paternalistic social relationships.

A spirituality of delight, however, does not give the immediate impression of being able to provide a sufficiently viable alternative to this "redemptionist" pattern of understanding, especially as the latter is generally assumed to be the traditional view. Yet there are at least two important reasons why it can do this. In the first place it should not be difficult to see that a spirituality of delight contains within itself the central affirmations of the Christian faith; namely, creation (original goodness), incarnation (social reordering), atonement ("letting-go and letting-be") and resurrection/spirit (delight). But although this spirituality may "contain" the central traditional doctrines, it is not couched in traditional terms. This is precisely because the traditional terminology has become a dead terminology for modern men and women. It is dead because it refuses now to release the truth which it once contained. It is no longer, as Rudolf Bultmann would have said, valid coin for us. It refuses to have an exchange value for what it once contained.

One of the major reasons for this is that the traditional doctrinal statements rely almost exclusively upon rationalist and voluntarist terminology, or belong, in terms of our attitudes towards them, to the world of mental concepts. They are couched in terms, or perceived to be couched in terms, which require the believer to give no more than rational assent to their truth. They are, either intrinsically or because we have made them so, part of the dominant rational world. The popular understanding of "believing" has become totally fideistic. It is seen to be a matter of accepting a number of apparently impossible and unprovable propositions as truth. Small wonder, therefore, that most people reject "belief" when it is presented to them in this way. The spirituality we have outlined seeks to redress the balance and begins with the actual affirmations of life which ordinary people can make – and in fact do make and live by a great deal of the time – and to discover the richer content of Christian theology which lies inherent within those affirmations. This is the *Via Positiva* which seeks to draw out from the natural what is supernatural by attention and contemplation, rather than by imposing what is supernatural upon what is natural (thereby implying that what is natural is not good) by reason and will.

The shift to a spirituality of delight is also important because it contains a shift in method. It constrains us to begin with experience and action, and to leave theological reflection until sundown. This is the method recommended by liberation theology.[2] We must proceed from an apprehension of the godwardness of ourselves and of all things, through a compassion which leads to the establishment of justice, allow ourselves along the way to be crucified by the loss of our false selves, and finally emerge into the desert of delight. The creation and exposition of theological systems, creeds even, is an activity for the end of the day, when all these other things have happened to us and we can, if we so desire, weave them together into a form of words. The important thing is that verbal theologizing happens last, and that true theology is "done" within us. The truth is being done within us and appropriated by us at the deepest levels of our being during the course of the day. When that has happened, when we are crucified and have risen again with Christ, when we have *lived* Christian doctrine within the community of faith active in the world, then we shall have the natural right to *speak* theologically.

A spirituality of delight, by placing goodness, trust, attention, wisdom and contemplation first, accepts this reversal of method. It accepts the need to begin with action and experience and to reflect upon it in the evening, in the complete trust that this reflection will actually bear a real resemblance to all the other reflections that have, so far, made up the life of the community in history (the tradition). By insisting on "belief" in the propositional sense before action, we have put the cart entirely before the horse. Human beings do not in reality live in that way. In the normal run of things we do not formulate our beliefs before we act. If we put belief before action we adopt a procedure which mistakes the status which doctrinal truths have. By doing that we actually fail to trust that the Christian affirmation is the truth about how it is with us as human beings. Christian doctrine is not just a set of opinions which some people happen to have, a series of discussable truths which may or may not be true, "an intellectual view", as it were. Christian truth is affirmed by Christians to be the truth about how it really is with human beings and with the world at the very deepest levels. Beneath the false selves and the illusions by which we live is the goodness of God, death and resurrection.

A spirituality of delight asks us to trust ourselves to that as being the case. If and when we do this we shall, at the end of the day, discover that we are "believers" and that the traditional theological affirmations which we thought we were unable to accept are now able to well up from within our depths. They will then be lived and "appropriated" truths, and we will be able to affirm them from within rather than simply acknowledge them as true, accepted by our minds but hardly by the whole self. But until we start from action we shall simply remain poor emaciated souls with a great deal of loose change in our pockets which we do not know what to do with.

That, in fact, is the state of the Church today. It is largely a collection of people with a number of beliefs rattling around in their pockets which they do not know how to translate into reality. It is small wonder that they wish to throw them away, and it is very easy for people like Don Cupitt, on the one hand, and extreme conservatives on the other, to make theological capital out of their condition. The point is not to throw the money away, nor to insist on using it as if everybody ought to know what it means. We must keep the money in our pockets and change the way we do things. The money will then, after we have changed the way we do things, by more readily able to regain its capacity to be a means of theological exchange and we will know which coins are valid and which are not. We must change the way we do things and construct our church life so that it contains a true affirmation of the goodness of creation, compassionate action for justice, letting go and letting be, wisdom, attention and contemplative prayer. Discovering how that can be done is not the task of this book. Once it is discovered, however, it will enable Christian doctrine to live again and regain its position as a true expression of what is going on. It will also enable the churches to relate far more closely to what is going on in society, rather than being so preoccupied with their own internal concerns. We can all be engaged in the struggle to establish goodness and justice where we are. The churches should be the points of focus, places of restoration in the struggle, areas of encouragement in these tasks. If they were then men and women would regain their ancient links with what the Church can be for them. If the churches can become once again the places where people actually do have the truth done within them, then the coinage of traditional Christian theology will become real, both for those within and for those without.

A spirituality of delight, therefore, is not simply a programme for the churches. It is also an invitation to all men and women. All of us are dislocated and out of joint because of our excessive reliance upon knowledge instead of wisdom, understanding instead of "seeing". We can only return to the good life by returning to our true selves in an acknowledgement of the delight that these selves can exhibit. In fact our true selves have usually been waiting for us to rely upon this delight for a long time. When we do we will find that reason and will will fall into place. They will not be abandoned but put to work in those areas where reason and will are appropriate, and be withdrawn when we are happily aware that they are inappropriate. At the moment we find that exercise extremely difficult. We lack confidence in our public lives and so give them over totally to reason and will. As a counterbalance we allow emotion to swamp our private existence as if emotion were the only thing appropriate in that sphere.

With greater confidence in the beauty and goodness of our whole created selves we could regain a wholeness to life, and the mind would be able to stand within the heart, which is where it actually stands in any case. Greater confidence that we are what Traherne calls "illustrious creatures" will be the beginning of our corporate good life. This would be confidence that who or what we are within is good, undivided, and given by God, that the pain we may have to bear will not destroy us, and that the delight we will be given will be, although not our own, enough to ravish us. When the middle classes of the Western world can "let go" enough to realize this then things may begin to change for the better. Communities may spring up in which these ideals are incorporated.[3] If so, well and good. Practical movements may be established in order to change the way things are done and bring them more into line with the elements of life we have outlined. If so we should join them. Revolutionary moments may occur in which deep-seated presuppositions are challenged and the strength of the mythologies which control us are revealed. What we do then will be governed by a number of factors, not the least being our attitude to violence if violence is involved. But nothing, absolutely nothing will occur until each person, within the silence of his or her own being, has been able to confront the depths of his or her own alienation and has learned to acknowledge, love, trust and delight in who they really are. They will certainly find much that they do not like, and a very great deal that they do not need, but further within they will find Christ the Word of God, co-creator with the Father, present from before the beginning, summoning them to trust and new life.

St Teresa of Avila compares the self to a great house with deep cellars. The cellars are full of bottles which have lain there for years unopened. They look dusty and dirty, covered in cobwebs and mould, and we may be tempted to throw them out. But if we lift them gently, open and pour them slowly, we shall be given the rich wine of the creation to drink.

The Good Life Regained

Notes

1. On the whole importance of "monastic eschatology" see also A. M. Allchin, *The World is a Wedding*, Darton, Longman and Todd, 1978. I have borrowed the phrase "interior" monasticism from the Orthodox theologian Paul Evdokimov, whose book, *The Struggle With God*, Paulist Press, New York, 1966, contains a number of parallels with my own work. I am grateful to Father Nicholas Behr for this reference.
2. See Gustavo Guttierez, *A Theology of Liberation*, Orbis, 1973, p. 11
3. There is, of course, a considerable literature on modern Christian communities and an interesting discussion in Stanley Hauerwas, *The Peaceable Kingdom*, SCM, 1983, chapter 6

Acknowledgement of Sources

The author is grateful for permission to use material from *The Sovereignty of Good* by Iris Murdoch, published in 1970 by Routledge and Kegan Paul, now Associated Book Publishers.

Some of his own material, originally prepared for various talks and seminars in Bristol, has previously been published as follows and is used by kind permission of the Journal of the Higher Education Foundation (parts of Chapters 1 and 2); *New Blackfriars* (chapter 5, slightly altered); and *Theology* (chapter 3, slightly altered).

Also available in Fount Paperbacks

BOOKS BY C. S. LEWIS

The Abolition of Man

'It is the most perfectly reasoned defence of Natural Law (Morality) I have ever seen, or believe to exist.'

Walter Hooper

Mere Christianity

'He has a quite unique power for making theology an attractive, exciting and fascinating quest.'

Times Literary Supplement

God in the Dock

'This little book . . . consists of some brilliant pieces . . . This is just the kind of book to place into the hands of an intellectual doubter . . . It has been an unalloyed pleasure to read.'

Marcus Beverley, Christian Herald

The Great Divorce

'Mr Lewis has a rare talent for expressing spiritual truth in fresh and striking imagery and with uncanny acumen . . . it contains many flashes of deep insight and exposures of popular fallacies.'

Church Times

I Believe
Trevor Huddleston

A simple, prayerful series of reflections on the phrases of the Creed. This is a beautiful testament of the strong, quiet inner faith of a man best known for his active role in the Church — and in the world.

The Heart of the Christian Faith
Donald Coggan

The author ". . . presents the essential core of Christianity in a marvellously simple and readable form, quite uncluttered by any excess of theological technicality."

The Yorkshire Post

Be Still and Know
Michael Ramsey

The former Archbishop of Canterbury looks at prayer in the New Testament, at what the early mystics could teach us about it, and at some practical aspects of Christian praying.

Pilgrim's Progress
John Bunyan

"A masterpiece which generation after generation of ordinary men and women have taken to their hearts."

Hugh Ross Williamson

Fount Paperbacks

Fount is one of the leading paperback publishers of religious books and below are some of its recent titles.

☐ GETHSEMANE Martin Israel £2.50
☐ HIS HEALING TOUCH Michael Buckley £2.50
☐ YES TO LIFE David Clarke £2.95
☐ THE DIVORCED CATHOLIC Edmund Flood £1.95
☐ THE WORLD WALKS BY Sue Masham £2.95
☐ C. S. LEWIS: THE MAN AND HIS GOD
   Richard Harries £1.75
☐ BEING FRIENDS Peter Levin £2.95
☐ DON'T BE AFRAID TO SAY YOU'RE LONELY
   Christopher Martin £2.50
☐ BASIL HUME: A PORTRAIT Tony Castle (ed.) £3.50
☐ TERRY WAITE: MAN WITH A MISSION
   Trevor Barnes £2.95
☐ PRAYING THROUGH PARADOX Charles Elliott £2.50
☐ TIMELESS AT HEART C. S. Lewis £2.50
☐ THE POLITICS OF PARADISE Frank Field £3.50
☐ THE WOUNDED CITY Trevor Barnes £2.50
☐ THE SACRAMENT OF THE WORD Donald Coggan £2.95
☐ IS THERE ANYONE THERE? Richard MacKenna £1.95

All Fount paperbacks are available through your bookshop or newsagent, or they can be ordered by post from Fount Paperbacks, Cash Sales Department, G.P.O. Box 29, Douglas, Isle of Man. Please send purchase price plus 22p per book, maximum postage £3. Customers outside the UK send purchase price, plus 22p per book. Cheque, postal order or money order. No currency.

NAME (Block letters)_____

ADDRESS _____

_____

_____

While every effort is made to keep prices low, it is sometimes necessary to increase them at short notice. Fount Paperbacks reserve the right to show new retail prices on covers which may differ from those previously advertised in the text or elsewhere.